RELIGIOUS BELIEF AND PRACTICES

(A Portrayal of the Integrative Process)

RELIGIOUS BELIEF AND PRACTICES

(A Portrayal of the Integrative Process)

Amitabha Sarkar
M.Sc. Ph.D

Samira Dasgupta
M.Sc, Ph.D.

AGAM KALA PRAKASHAN
NEW DELHI

First Published 2010

ISBN : 978-81-7320-094-6

Published by
Dr. Agam Prasad, M.A., Ph.D., Diploma in Museology
For **Agam Kala Prakashan**
34, Central Market, Ashok Vihar, Delhi-110 052.
Ph. : 011-27212195, 47098550, 65688806-7
Fax : 011-27212195
E-mail : agambooks@gmail.com, agambook@yahoo.com

Composed by
Elegant Printographics
319, IIIrd Floor, R. G. Complex,
Sector-14, Rohini, Delhi-110085

Printed at
Chawla Offset Printers
Delhi-110052.

Printed in India

CONTENTS

PREFACE

To our mind religion is a phenomenon of social articulation followed by ritual and practices and by practicing it one have to feel security from uncertainty as well as feeling of an in-group social bondage, which differs from others. The intricate dependence upon various benevolent and malevolent spirits, which becomes the part and parcel of survival strategy in a particular ecological niche signifies a kind of belief and dependence towards Supreme Being in the celestial world. The present treatise highlights the religiosity of Bastar tribal groups who are having their own territorial boundary but the role of mother cult –Mata Danteshwari – the tutelary deity of Bastar King, acts like a centripetal force where both Hindu and Tribal are roaming from apex to center. The also acts as a cohesive social unit through which distant pargana and villages of Bastar are tied up through a single thread. Apart from this we consider Lakshmi Jagar ritual is in between foraging hunter-gatherer stage to settled agricultural group and till date practice by peasaut community (that is, in between tribe and caste) incorporating many Sanskritic tenets.

Further, the social mobility movement is very much found among the Bhatra tribal group and for this we were much inspired due to our office colleague—Sri Sahedeo who himself was a Bhatra. For collection of data on this aspect he acted as a field guide and interpreter to us.

The interest of this sort of work instilled to us during our official posting at Jagdalpur from 1991 to 1998 in Anthropological Survey of India. We had ample opportunities during the period to have a close observation on the life and culture of tribal people in and around Jagdalpur. The present volume is absolutely based on direct involvement in field investigation in several of their ritual activities in the villages. Collection of empirical data in various locales essentially requires getting information on time and personal and timely visit to the places of occurrences, which are, spread over throughout the Bastar district (undivided).

At the very outset, we owe a deep debt of gratitude to all the informants and district administration for their full-fledged co-operation in collecting data as well as arranging our accommodation in remote and sensitive areas of Bastar. We consider it is our sacred duty to convey our sincere regards to all of them.

We also express our thanks to Sri, Asok Mukhopadhyay and Dr.G.K.Bera for their active involvement in data collection during Dusehra festival of Jagdalpur on 2004. We are grateful to Sri,Santosh Pathak and Debashis Biswas of Anthropological Survey of India, Kolkata for their painstaking effort in typing the manuscript in the computer as well as digital conversion of our coloured photographs.

We shall be failing in our duty if we do not acknowledge with respect to Dr.Biman K Dasgupta, ex. Deputy Director of Anthropological Survey of India who guided us a lot in preparing this manuscript. We are also grateful to Director, Anthropological survey of India, who inspired us in many ways to conduct and carry out fundamental field oriented research with valuable publication. Special thanks are due to Dr.Agam Prasad of Agam Kala Prakashan, a prestigious publishing house of Delhi, for the specific care and attention given by him to bring out this book in such a short time. Lastly, we think our endeavour would meet a profound success if requisite interest is developed among the researchers and planners in this field to understand the present day Bastar tribal situation where Danteshwari Mata plays a key and decisive role even at their local developmental issue.

Chapter-1

Introduction

A set of beliefs, emotional attitudes etc. when practice by a group of people in order to cope up with his surrounding unknown and unseen problems which is otherwise termed as supernatural power, - is identified as religion. Religion is a universal and pervasive institution in human life. The belief, thought and action with which religion is concerned could be found at all levels of culture i.e. among technologically ill developed marginalized tribal communities or even in advanced group of civilized people.

Herbert Spencer develops the theory of ghost worship by dealing elaborately with the primitive idea of life, death, resurrection, soul, spirit, the other world and the cult of the ghost. Spencer finds that some notion of existence beyond death, however vague, is almost universal. Perhaps from this belief comes the idea of ghost propitiation, not only at the time of funeral but also on various events. According to Spencer the seed of regular ancestor worship originates from here and he also opined that root of every religion may be traced from ancestor worship, and all other forms such as idol worship, fetish worship, nature, animal, plant etc. worship, develop out of ancestor worship. In fact we do not find any society without religious beliefs and practices. All religion consist of a mental attitude which is in the shape of beliefs and rituals; the former is regarded as the static part, while the latter as the dynamic part of religion. According to Banerjee (1990) " what differentiates the so called higher religious from the primitive varieties is the relative absence of philosophical speculation in the latter... The whole primitive 'philosophy' is called animism and the system of primitive ideas is constituted by so called magic". According to Durkheim (1954) there are two component elements in the supernatural belief, that is, sacred as religion while profane part as magic or primitive science.

Religion, concerned as it is with shared beliefs and practices, is pre-eminently social and until modern times was to be found universally in every human society. The central interest of religion appears to concern something comparatively vague and intangible, whose empirical reality is far from clear. It is concerned with a "beyond", with man's relation to and attitude towards that "beyond" for human life. (O'dea, 1969).

According to functional theory culture is a more or less integrated body of knowledge, pseudo-knowledge, beliefs and values. Culture, understood in this way, is a symbolic system of meaning, some of which define reality, as it is believed to be, others of which define normative expectations incumbent on humans. The elements making up the system of cultural meaning may be either implicit or explicit. Culture is integrated with the social system in that it enters into the definition of means and ends, of proscriptions and prescriptions, of the permitted and the forbidden, by defining the roles within which a society's members confront the established expectations of their social situation. Religion with its transcendent reference to a beyond, is an important aspect of this cultural phenomenon. Culture is the creation by man of a world of adjustment and meaning, in the context of which human life can be significantly lived. (O'dea 1969).

Functional theory sees the contribution of religion to human societies and cultures to be based upon its central characteristic; its transcendence of everyday experience in the natural environment. Functional theory demands such needs as the result of three fundamental characteristics of human existence.

First, man lives in conditions of uncertainty; events of crucial significance to his safety and welfare are beyond his prevision. Human existence, in other words, is characterized by contingency.

Second, man's capacity to control and affect the condition of his life, although increasing, is inherently limited. At a certain point, man's condition with respect to the conflict between his wants and his environment is characterized by powerlessness.

Third, men must live in a society, and a society is an orderly allocation of functions, facilities and rewards. It involves both a division of labour and a division of product. It requires imperative coordination- that is, some degree of super ordination and subordination in the relation of men. Moreover, societies exist amid condition of scarcity – the third fundamental characteristic of human existence.

Thus it reveals that the role of religion as assisting men to adjust to the speechless facts of contingency, powerlessness and scarcity. These are existential characteristics of the human condition in terms of functional theory and are therefore inherent to some degree in all-human societies. Religion in these terms is seen as the most basic "mechanism" of adjustment to the aleatory and frustrating elements (O'dea 1969).

II

The social function of religion is articulation among its members as well as imposing some values, which lead the society to an ordered existence and continuing system of relationship amongst its members in harmonious way.

Malinowski (1948) considers religions as the device to secure mental and psychical stability in one individual's life. It has been originated to bring about a re-adjustment between man and the supernatural in upset states of existence, while to Radcliffe-Brown (1935) religion has been originated just as a means for social survival that is, out of a sense of dependence on it. It is the fear of supernatural. According to Tylor (1871) religion means the belief in spiritual beings. Tylor's three major propositions on the origin and development of human religion also received empirical support, viz, (a) religion developed out of fear (b) though the conservatives think that religion is the product of civilization, yet there are suitable ordeal that all the societies of the world (advanced or archaic/simple) have their won interpretation of religion, which is not much diverse so far the core matter is concerned (c) all religions consist of a mental attitude and dependence towards the supernatural power.

Religion is said to be born out of physical and social needs. Early men lived under the sky open either in hills or forests and had to pass through some uncertainty and totally dependent at the mercy of nature. In course of maintaining livelihood which was full of struggle for existence in such a precarious condition of environment they were forced to depend on some supernatural power in order to revamp their minds to get requisite courage for overcoming the surrounding woes. Even today when one is in obscure state he or she usually seeks the help from supernatural power to overcome the crisis in life. In a way this is religious belief system, which usually acts as a dependable walking stick like that of a blind man. The things, which are beyond our control, can be achieved by depending on supernatural power. It is also to be mentioned that religion helps to integrate not only the society but also the personality (Davis, Kingsley, 1966).

There are two ways of expression of supernaturalism or belief in supernatural power.

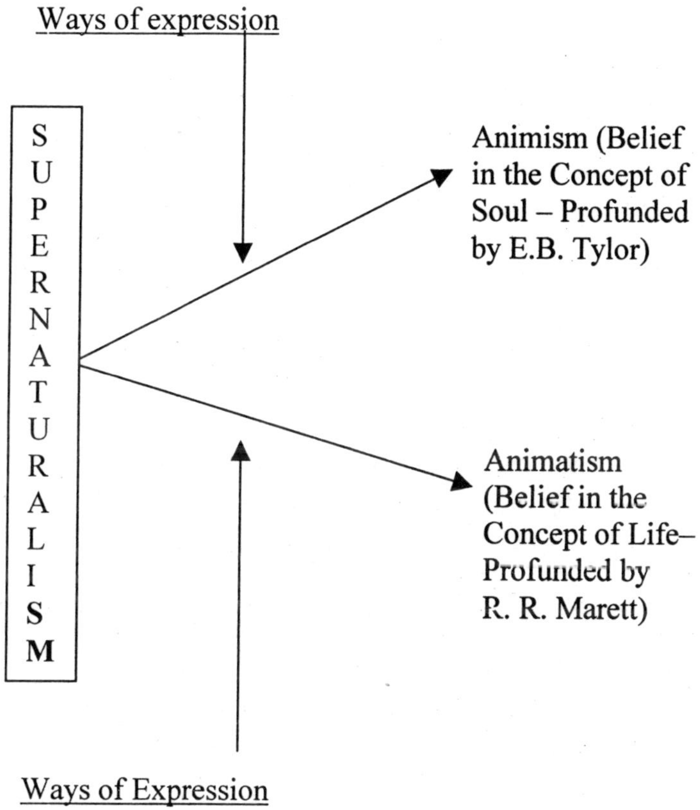

Animism

According to Tylor (1871) the origin of animism is from the phenomenon of dreams and also of life and death. The forest devellers, primitives or autochthous could not discover any physical difference between and living and a dead man excepting perception of heartbeat from outside. Considering this Tylor opined that the early men believed something is active in the living body and in the absence of such active rhythmic feeling, it could not function any activities like a living person. Thus the concept of soul was established. The soul is the cause of life and thought. Absence of such soul leads to an end of an individual. The Ho of Singhbhum believe that when a man dies, some ethrial substance leaves the body. It is the soul. Some articles are put in the graves in the belief that the departed soul of celestial world will use those. The Ho who cremate the body, put the personal belongings of the deceased on his pyre. Similarly Abujh Maria of Bastar put the personal belongings of deceased on the surface of grave; it has been observed that personal belongings of deceased like transistor, wristwatch, umbrella etc were left on the surface of grave. The Ho usually call back the soul at the *ading* after a few days. "Ading" is the sacred place for the ancestral spirits. The Birjias of Chotanagpur also call back the soul (*mua*) after a few days of death at their sacred place in the room – *ora bhitar*, where outsiders are tabooed to enter (Dasgupta, 1994). The Dhodia of South Gujarat also belief in such soul and after death they usually inserted a wooden small log (*khatrun*) in the backside corner of their household (Sarkar, 1994). The new soul thus becomes the ancestral spirit and lives there till reincarnation. Thus, the concept of soul is the foundation of animism.

Animatism

It is concerned with a tendency to enrich even inanimate nature with a life similar to that in himself and his equals. It is present in primitive savage and advanced societies. The former group worships inanimate nature while the latter attaches special quality to inanimate things like amulet, *tabiz*, ring affixed with precious/semi-precious stone which are supposed to possess the amazing power to control unfavourable events as well as stars and planets.

To a primitive mind, it is the spirit of nature that works. The tribal religon is found having faith in supernatural power in bones and feathers etc. This impersonal power is worshipped to maintain peace and prosperity in the group. Often it is difficult to differentiate between animatism and animism. However, according to animatism there lies some mysterious, unknown, impersonal power at the back of all living beings while things according to animism there is spirit found in all movable and immovable objects. The examples of animatism are found among the tribal peoples of Chotanagpur Plateau and also among the Bastar tribe like Muria, Abujh Maria, Dorla, Bison-Horn Maria, Bhatras, Halba, Gadaba and Dhurwa etc. They consider the bones, beads, stones and feathers (especially of peacock) to have living and magical powers. The stones are considered to be children of earth goddess or *dharti mai* or *tallur mutte* (among Murias of Bastar) and worshipped. It has been observed that usually tribal people worship only those powers, which are functional to their sustainable living condition.

Mana

The term 'mana' originates from Melanesian term, means power. Mana is a force but not the vitalistic force. It exists as a supernatural attributes of persons and things. Extra-ordinary aptitudes of man are often explained interms of mana. This power does not follow the regular laws of nature. Like animism it transcends the natural i.e. some mysterious power is attached to them and that is the reason why mana is supernatural.

Thus, religion is instinctive to man. Man is the only religious being. Man is the finite-infinite being. From the time when he opened his eyes on this earth, he has been desirous of knowing and being acquitted with the conscious power latent in nature. As and when he was compelled to face natural hardships, dangers, storms, floods, lightning, famines, epidemics, scarcity in any resource for sustenance, dreaded animals etc, man has looked upto some invisible power for assistance, motivation, strength and help. Therefore, this religious tendency awoke in man when he was gripped sometimes by fear and at other times by curiosity. In this way, man time and again attempted to quench his urges in that Supreme person – the search of which is religion.

III

Bastar (undivided) is a region where people of various cultures lived together, often sharing each other's cultural traits. Bastar can be compared with a bowl where various ethnic groups especially tribes such as Abujh Maria, Murias, Dandamin Maria, Bhatra, Halba, Dhurwa and Dorla live with their individual identity with its own religious beliefs and practices which in most cases have evolved in relation to particular environmentalbackground in which their habitat is located (Daspupta and Sarkar, 2003). Infact each of such tribal groups have some territorial demarcation in which they are distributed. Bastar is a forest clad zone, and inorder to live in such environment all the ethnic groups have adapted their life and culture accordingly and practise various rituals and festivals. Life in Bastar is a mosaic of colourful happenings. The festivals are not mere occasions but deep-rooted traditions and customs woven into the fabric of socio-cultural life of Bastar and thus a harmonious co-existence among different ethnic groups castes, tribes prevails.

India is a vast country with many languages, religions and ways of life. These different cultures like different flowers composing and colourful bunch have merged to one single entity, namely the Indian Civilization (Banerjee, 1968).

Therefore, to study the rituals and festivals of Bastar, will clearly reveal a mirror picture of life style and culture of Bastar people, which is chiefly, dominated by tribes. A festival is a social institution, which provides an occasion for individual or communal worship of different deities, it is a place for meeting with friends and relatives, wearing of some special new clothes, as well as eating of special food, merry making, visit of fairs and purchase of essential items etc. The primary theme of a festival is religious one. It can also be said that a festival has two dimensions, namely, sacred and secular. The sacred performances are held to please supernatural power either individually or communally as a welfare measure while, secular aspect of a festival consists of drinking, eating, singing, dancing, merry making, social visits enjoying the fair etc.

The idea of religion comes from the potentiality of a power which is conceived as superior to man and hence directs and controls his activities (Joshi, 1986). Thus, religion may be described as a system of beliefs and practices towards 'ultimate concern' of a society. "Ultimate concern", a concept used by Paul Tillich, has two aspects – meaning and power viewed in this way religion is concerned with the explanation and expression of the words, it has important integrative functions for groups and for individual personalities. At the same time religion is concerned with the threats to these central values or to social or individual existence, it has important defense functions managing tensions and anxieties (Lessa and Vogt, 1965).

Area of Study

The data of the present treatise were collected from Bastar district (undivided) chiefly during 1991 to 1999 from Jagadalpur, Narayanpur, Orcha, Bhopalpatnam, Bijapur, Bakawand, Sukma, Bacheli, Konta, Erabore (near Konta) area and also from its neighbouring villages. During data collection Bastar district was not divided into three parts viz., Dantewada, Kanker and Bastar. Now, many field investigating area are not in Bastar district proper. Therefore, all along in the text we have considered Bastar district as an undivided unit of universe of present study. Also during 2004 data on Dusehra festival were collected at Jagdalpur in order to understand its syncretic nature as well as a kind of centripetal force in action.

Objective

In the present treatise authors try to highlight about the religiosity of tribal groups who are territorially demarcated with individual identity. In the participation of various worship and festivals the author have tried to arsen how various ethnic groups are involved and function for common interest. The festivals which are of syncretic in nature or a platform of cultural synthesis brings various ethnic groups together for common interest which on all occasion found to appease mother goddess cult who possesses a centripetal force of action among the various ethnic groups. Lastly, on each belief and practices among the ethnic groups of Bastar possesses a deep-rooted sentaiment attached with their value system for their sustenable living. Infact their belief in supernatural powers for maintaining their livelihood in such forest clad environment, directly speak for uncertainity of living condition. This also reveals their backwardness even in this space era or an era of globalization. Due to close association of various ethnic groups they have developed a kind of tolerance and respect to each other as well as adaptation and assimilation of various cultural traits among themselves due to survival strategy. Centering around such strategy which acts like a cohesive agent and this function as a centripetal force through which all the communities are integrated which result fusion of cultural behaviour and religious snthesis in Bastar. Parctise of occultism is very common in Bastar, which also sign for backwardness.

Methodology

Data were collected from each tribal group who are settled in undivided Bastar district and their settlement pattern is territorially segmented. Along with this data were collected from the chief festivals of Bastar as a participant observer in which all the ethnic groups were involved to perform their assigned jobs. Village level data were also taken to understand the role of various local mother goddess cults and its network of relation with the pantheon of great tradition. The standard anthropological tools and techniques have been applied in collection of data. All the data were collected from1991 to 1998 during our period of posting and also during 1999 and 2004.

Chapter-2

Ethno-Historical Account and People

The landmass of the district is quite ancient but its early history is in obscurity and very little about the area has come to light. Whatever little is known about the history of Bastar is by way of chronological reconstruction of events on the basis of inferences drawn from Sanskrit literature, contemporary rock inscriptions and sporadic researches based on copper plates and coins etc. found almost inadvertently in the region. It is also claimed that during the period of early history Dandak was known as Chakrakut, which included some portions of Jeypore region of present day Orissa state. The area of about 2500 sq.miles comprising Kotpad, Churchuneda, Rodagarh, Umarkot, Hamir Raigarh of Jeypore princely state was part of Chakrakut and continued to be the part of Bastar till the advent of British Rule in the area.

Bastar has experienced a number of historical waves, which have resulted into diverse cultural mosaic in this area. The Nals established kingdom during mid 6th century followed by dark era for about 5 years followed by Chalukyas and Ganga kings of Orissa. Then Nagvanshi king came. They started their reign from middle of 11th century to 14th century. Then it was under control of Chalukyas of Godavari region and Annam Deo was the first Kakatiya king of Chalukya dynasty. The book "Maria

Gonds of Bastar" by Grigson (1991 reprinted) accepts Annam Deo to have established his princely rule in Bastar in 1323 A.D. With the beginning of Annam Deo's rule Chakrakot came to be known as Bastar (Glasfurd, 1862). The family of the Raja of Bastar is ancient and is said to have come from Warangal of Andhra Pradesh at about 1323 A.D. when Muslim invaded the area and caused these rulers to flee from there towards north of Godavari. According to the traditions of the family, Annam Deo established himself in Bastar under the protection and grace of their tutelary deity – Danteshwari. In 1853 it came into direct political relations with the British. The last king in the line was Pravir Chandra Bhanjdeo who ruled the state till its merger with Madhya Pradesh. It is also reported from historical accounts that during the Purushottam Deo's regime (1468-1534) the capital was shifted to the northern side of the river Indravati and named the newly established capital at Bastar. Bastar is situated 28 km away from Jagdalpur town and now it has become a large village. The most memorable event in the context of present discourse was his visit to Lord Jagannath at Puri of Orissa. He visited Puri by crawling in spite of having elephants, horses and Chariot etc. He to show respect to Lord Jagannath. He was the first Kakatiya king who visited the deity/shrine. Seeing his devotion Lord Jagannath became very much pleased and ordered the local king and priest of the temple through his divine command to invite Raja Purushottam. They gave him warm reception and entertained him as chief guest. On his return he was offered a Chariot with sixteen wheels. Among the 16 wheels Raja Purushottam offered back four wheels to Lord Jagannath and returned to Bastar with the rest 12 wheels along with group of Barhai (carpenter) who used to make chariot and a group of Aranyak Brahman priest. The rest 12 wheels were offered to their family tutelary deity – Devi Danteshwari. He started the festival of *rath parikrama* at Bastar during Dusehra. The 12 wheels make two chariots; one of those with four wheels and another with rest eight wheels. These two chariots namely, *Phool rath* and *raini rath* go round in Jagdalpur town during dusehra and this tradition is continued till date. At that time the King used to sit on the chariot with their own family deity – Devi Danteshwari (Sarkar and Dasgupta, 1996, Sundar, 1997).

The Maharaja as head of the state carried out the administration of Bastar State and a Diwan assisted him. The Diwan had powers of a District and session Judge and he carried out his functions with the assistance of two subordinate judges. The Tehsildars and Managers had powers of Munasiff and were enjoying the powers of a second class Magistrate. The state was divided into five tehsils viz., Narayanpur, Kondagaon, Jadgalpur, Bijapur and Konta and four Zamindaris viz. Kutru, Bhoopalpatnam, Pamed and Sukuma. Mr Chapman wrote in 1898 that the whole state was divided into about eighty eight (88) parganas that were under paid officials who exercised civil and criminal powers besides collecting land revenue. Again in a *pargana* there are several villages under its control. A list of such *pargana* is given to understand the network of relation from the King to village at grass root level. The wild and distant parganas were for purposes of revenue collection under **Thanedars, Negis or Hikmis**. These officials were paid officers and they had under them paid servants who received a monthly payment. (Jay, 1970). It is reported that *Thanaedars* were responsible for collection of taxes from distant parganas; *Negi* was a lesser person who had control over a number of villages; while *Hikmis* was employed under *Negi* to help collect revenue. Under *Hikmis* there was several village headman and taxes apparently were collected from Headman of village who were responsible for the person in their respective communities.

The unit of land measurement was *nagar* representing the area of land that could be kept under cultivation with a pair of bullocks during one season. A plough was considered to be equal to 10 to 12 acres. Periodical assessment was made by collecting information from neighbouring village about the number of cattle used by each cultivator in the area. Money was practically unknown and all the payments were not made in kind but were paid in cowries. The rate of assessment throughout the state used to be five *dogani* of cowries, which is equivalent to 50 paisa per plough. A rupee as a currency was first introduced in the state in about 1865 when teak, timber of the district found a market to Madras (Singh Deo, 1984).

Therefore, it appears that the King of the Bastar State has easy access to articulate with his subalterns even in distant wild area of the state through the system of land revenue collection or *pargana manjhi* system. In fact *pargana manjhi* has a vital role in the state that acted as a liaison between state administration and villagers at the grass root level.

The Names Of Bastar Kings

1. Annam Deo (1323-1369)
2. Hamir Deo (1369-1410)
3. Bhairab Deo (1410-1468)
4. Purusotham Deo (1468-1534)
5. Jaising Deo (1534-1558)
6. Narsing Deo (1558-1602)
7. Pratapraj Deo (1602-1625)
8. Jagdishraj Deo (1625-1639)
9. Virnaryan Deo (1639-1654)
10. Virsing Deo (1654-1680)
11. Dikpal Deo (1680-1709)
12. Rajpal Deo (1709-1721)
13. Chandel (1721-1731)
14. Dalpat Deo (1731-1774)
15. Ajmer Sing (1774-1777)
16. Dariya Deo (1777-1800)

17. Mahipal Deo(1800-1842)

Bhopal Deo (1842—1853) | Lal Dalganjan Singh

Bhairam Deo (1853—1891) = Jujraj Kaur

= Subran Kaur (Senior Rani in 1910)

= Kundan Kaur

Rudra pratap Deo (1891—1922)

Maharani Prafulla Kumari = Prafulla Kumar of Mayurbhanj, Orissa
(1922—1936)

Kamla | Pravir Chandra = Vedvati (1936—1948, died 1968) | Gita | Vijay = Hitendra Kumari

Bharat = Krishna
(Adopted by Pravir)

Kamal Ch.Bhanjdeo--- present Raja coronated on 19-9-96

List of Parganas of undivided Bastar District

Sl. No.	Name of Parganas	Sl.No.	Name of Parganas
1.	Kesarpal	46	Sonarpal
2.	Amawal	47	Baragaon
3.	Mingachal (Sub-Zamindari-Gudma)	48	Dugal
4.	Alwar (Sub-Zamindari -Toynar)	49	Benur
5.	Dudepalli	50	Karangal
6.	Kutru	51	Naryanpur
7.	Bhairamgarh	52	Chote Dongar
8.	Marian Lanka	53	Dantewara
9.	Pharasgarh (Sub-Zamindari Pharasgarh)	54	Kuvakonda
10.	Pesewara (Sub-Zamindari – Pesewara	55	Katekalyan
11.	Chindgarh	56	Kavali
12.	Hamirgarh	57	Pinamera
13.	Korramanka	58	Ilmeri
14.	Kerlapal	59	Pedamera
15.	Bhopalpatnam	60	Barsur
17	Lingapur	61	Kilepal
18.	Madder	62	Mandhota
19.	Chandur	63	Korramanka
20	Lingagiri	64	Amirgarh
21.	Mirtur Pargana	65	Chintaluar
22	Magnar	66	Konta
23.	Pamer	67	Phutkal
24.	Kotpalli	68	Pharsal
25.	Kachora	69	Bardal
26.	Agarwara	70	Pharsigotal
27.	Tirathgarh	71	Tula gotul

28.	Chitrakot	72	Kolar
29.	Garhia	73	Hukka-gotal
30.	Chitpur	74	Nurdesh
31.	Yerpund	75	Jatwar
32.	Karekot	76	Patal desh
33.	Raykera	77	Bademar
34.	Panchgaon	78	Chhotemar
35.	Bara Gaon	79	Sonpur
36.	Jaitgiri	80	Bandadesh
37.	Amora	81	Pratappur
38.	Marpal	82	Kalpatti
39.	Kaikagarh	83	Kirangal
40.	Hatiya	84	Antagarh
41.	Sonawal	85	Amabera
42.	Amraoti	86	Bhomra
43.	Charke	87	Koilibira
44	Bamhni	88	Surewahi
45	Kongur		

The People

The Bastar (undivided) district of Chhattishgarh is tribal infested area with forest-clad environment. More than 75% population are tribal and they are chiefly Muria, Abujh Maria, Bhatra, Halba, Dandami Maria (or Bison-Horn Marai), Dorla, Dhurwa and a few pockets of Gadaba of the bordering Orissa belt. These tribal people are distributed sporadically in the district of which Abujh Maria are confined in north-western part, Dandami Maria are in south-central that is in Dantewada region while Muria are in north and north-west, Dorla are in southern part, that is, Konta region and western Bijapur area, Dhurwa are in south-eastern part of Kanger valley, Bhatra are confined in Indrawati plain in northern Jagadalpur while Halbas are distributed in north and south Bastar. All these tribal groups are endogamous in nature and possess own belief system, which are different from others and in this way ethnic boundary is maintained. Apart from these there are sizeable population of immigrants who are chiefly businessmen from Gujarat, Rajasthan, U.P.; there are also govt. employees and some pockets are dominated by Bengalee refugee settlements that were rehabilitated by the government in various parts of the district.

Chapter-3

Ethnic Background and Distribution

Bastar has been the meeting ground of the historical, linguistic and ancestral traditions of the states of Madhya Pradesh, namely, Orissa, Andhra and Maharashtra. Bastar is one of the large districts in our country. The approximate area of the district is 39175 square km. Bhopal is the capital of the state that is about 1000 km. Away from Bastar district head quarter – Jagadalpur. About 55% area of the district is still covered with forest and about 72% of the population are tribal. The influx of population in the district is gradually increasing. The original inhabitants of the district are tribal people, namely Abujh Maria, Dandami Maria, Muria, Bhatra, Halba, Dorla and Dhurwa. Apart from these there are other tribals, who are very small in number and more so, they are not the sons of soil of Bastar. About 20% of the population are businessmen (from Gujarat, Rajasthan and Uttar Pradesh), government service holders and Bengalee Refugees who are settled in various pockets of the district. Through empirical observation the author came to know that in general, economically these refugees population area lagging behind other non-tribal people in this area and could not improve themselves much inspite of their prolonged adjustment with the new geo-economic set up. These immigrant population re-interprets various of their traditional cultural repertoire in the new environment. The cultural pluralism have been noticed among immigrant population.

Now in the following lines the discussion will be on main tribal population of Bastar, their settlement and socio-cultural behaviour. The empirical observation reveals that these tribal groups are distributed in a particular territory of the forest clad Bastar district. Each tribal community has its own cultural boundary and within this cultural framework each group has to perform various kinds of socio-cultural behaviour which is typically their own. The Bastar tribes are classified under the generic name – Gond and they represent certain primitive stages and levels of development.

ABUJH MARIA

The Abujh Maria tribe lives entirely in Abujhmarh hills. This belt extends from Kutru to Barsur and southwards beyond Bhairamgarh west of Kutru, are characterized by mixed Hill Maria with Dorla and these Hill Marias have almost become Dorla. Among the Abujhmaria clans (Katta) are unilinear descent groups. Each clan has a clan god [Pen] whom they worship. All the members of a clan believe that they are descended from a common ancestor. A group of different clans [Katta] are called bhaiband or dadabhai [brother-clan] and marital alliance in those having bhaiband relationship is prohibited, and alongwith this they also practise clan exogamy. They are permitted to settle marriage only with a member of wife's clan, called akomam. Therefore, all the clans have some bhaiband clans and some akomam clan. The situation cannot be understood by saying only clan exogamy or phratry exogamy system. Among the Hill Maria, they have knowledge about every clan either brother's or a wife's clan. A person among them is allowed to acquire mate from wife clan [akomama] only. They are patrilocal and prefer cross-cousing marriage.

Bride price system is prevalent. Monogamy is the rule. Polygyny is also allowed. Marriage by negotiation [pendul] is the rule and marriage rituals are performed by their community elders. The other form of acquiring mate lamareh [marriage by service, gharjamai, vitte [marriage by elopment], koheberdan [marriage by exchange], aeohundi [junior levirate], koyeyari [sororrate] and widow marriage are also allowed. The date of marriage is fixed adjusting with the local market day. Divorce is discouraged. They bury the dead and the belonging of the deceased are kept and a stone slab or menhir, locally known as mengrahal is erected on the burial. They are mainly penda cultivators, though they also practice incipient form of settled cultivation. Their tradition council is headed by pargana manjhi assisted by a village Patel. It deals with the disputes between the members of the community. They believe in animism. They worship their clan deities. Kaksar is their chief festival, performed in the month of June. The abujh Maria considers Kaksar [a festival of dance] and Kudin as the harvest festivals and also a new eating ceremony for all the crops but its main purpose seems to be to honour the clan gods before the beginning of the monsoon and resume of hard labour in their cultivable land.

MURIA

The east of Abujhmarh hills that is, the remaining part of Narayanpur tehsil including its southern portion is a belt of Jhoria Muria or Muria. They are low landers or plain Muria who apparently belong to same stock of Hill Maria although they maintain endogamy. The abode of Muria tribe is Kondagaon tehsil, north Narayanpur and northcentral part of Jagadalpur. The Muria young boys wear white cloth above the knees and wear turban on their head. They tie a headband with long string of beads on it. Combs are tucked into the folds of the turban. They keep chutta [leafpipe] and chunoti [tobacco box] in its folds. They tie their hairs at the back with a bunch of feathers or tassels or red wool. They wear various kinds of bead ornaments.

Regarding their social organization and clan system it is very much similar with they of Abujhmaria. That is, they also possess phratry system. The clan of other pratries with whom marital relations can be established known as akomama. Each phratry consists of severals clans, who have totem such as clan buji [bullock-a-totem], dhurwa [goat], wika [kassi tree], sori/sodi [tiger] bod [a kind of sish] etc. The phartry and the clans are exogamous in nature. Monogamy and adult marriage are the rule but polygyny is also permitted. They have a custom of bride price. Marriage by negotiations [ful kochna] is most prefered and cross cousin marriage is also prefered. Apart from these, there are several other types of acquiring of, mate that are allowed such as, ostasana marmi, talk dayna, arwitana, hai wark wat, tika tasana and yer dosana amrmi. Divorce is permitted. They have ghotul system that they consider as sacred place and they never do any sin there. According to their legend Lingo pen was the creator of ghotul. They have a belief on the supreme Being called – Mahaprabhu, Ispural and Bhagwan. Songur mate is their one of the important goddess. The earth is regarded as their mother goddess. Their rain god is known as Bhimul. The Muria priests and sacred specialists are Kaizer, Gaita, pen gaita and pujar. They have also gunnia. These posts are hereditary. They have their own social council headed by Manjhi, which is hereditary post. He wears red turban and he is assisted by patel.

DANDAMI MARIA

The Bison-Horn Maria or Dandami Maria are primarily the inhabitants of Dantewada tehsil which is an enclosed basin and extends over the surrounding plateau and lowlands for some distance like the Indrawati river of the north, Dubbatota on the south, Chitrakote, Tirathgarh, Tongpal and Sukma in the east and Bijapur, Basaguda on the west. The enclosed basin of Bison-Horn Maria was almost isolated from the urban people of the surrounding area but with the advent of NMDC iron mining area, this area is becoming changed due to impact of industrialization. The central part of Konta tehsil i.e. from Basaguda to Dubatota form a transition belt between Bison Horn Maria on the north east and Dorla in the south-west. Infact, this area is admixture of Dorla and Bison-Horn Maria, which is again exposed to Telugu influence. They donot have any ghotul system. Their musical dancing instruments are 'dhol' for men and jhumka lathi-iron dancing stick for women. During dance the male wear a typical headgear of horn headdress, for which they are called as Bison-Horn Maria.

They are divided into a number of exogamous, totemintic phratries or bans namely, Marri, Kuhrami, Sodi, Markami and Kawasi. Again, each of them is divided into a number of exogamous, toteminstic clan [katta]. The main' function of phratry and clan is to regulate marriage. The word dadabhai is used to designate kindred or brother clan with whom marriage is prohibited. Gudupal or cross-cousin marriage is preferred. As per their customary law marriage takes place at their early ages before puberty. It is known as mangin. After puberty, the actual marriage ceremony is performed. Divorce is permitted. Their economic life revolves around land and forest. A Pedda heads their own jati panchayat of socal control. This is hereditary post. Para Mukhia, Kotwar and Aut Paharia assist him. Apart from this they have inter-village organization or pargana panchayat, headed by pargana Manjhi. The outskirt of every Dandami Maria village is the abode of their clan god who is believed as a protector of the territory in which their clan members reside. They worship earth goddess Bhum regarded as their mother goddess who feeds and sustains her Maria children.

DORLA

The Dorla, aother major tribal group of Bastar live in Godavari-Sabri river low lands in western Bijapur tehsil and southern Konta. Their immediate neighbours in the south are the Koya [in Orissa] and the Hill Reddi [in A.P.] and in the north and north-west are the Bison-Horn Maria and the Hill Maria. It is also reported that Dorla of Konta area often made marital alliace with Koya of Malkangiri, Orissa, often they are known as Dor-Koi or Koya. Infact, river Sabari is the demarcation line of two adjoining states, i.e., Madhya Pradesh and Orissa, where Dorla settlement is found. Their house type is typical, it is thatched with four slopes with a front verandah.

They are strictly endogamous group, having number of exogamous phratries or gatta Viz., Paremboi, Paren, Muro, Aido and Erogatta. Again, each gatta consists of number of inteperu or clan and each intiperu possess a Pen or clan god. Monogamy is the rule but polygyny is not discouraged. Married women wear a particular kind of necklace known as pustetadu as a symbol of marriage. They are basically settled cultivators. Personal possession of palm tree is a kind of status symbol in their society. They have their own traditional council of social control, headed by a Patel Majhi and Dhurwa and a Bandhroth assists him. They believe in the existence of spirits of natural objects such as hills, jungle, water etc. and also in ghosts and other malevolent spirits. They also worship the souls of their ancestors. They are in believe of black magic. They also observe number of festivals or pandums which are closely woven with their agricultural activities, and other related things through which their subsistence pattern is deeply involved; they are Bija Pandum, Tarn Pandum, Sukur Pandum, Kossra Pandum, Bhimin Pandum etc. From Konta through river Sabri, bamboos are transported to Andhra, which is a typically indigenous method. Many Dorla labourers are engaged in bamboo harvesting in forest.

DHURWA

The Dhurwa [or Parja] live in Southern-Eastern Jagdaipur tehsil and part of Sukma Revenue Inspector's circle. Their distribution also extends eastwards into the adjacent Koraput district of Orissa. They have assumed the name Dhurwa which is more prestigious than Parja-a synonym. Culturally, the Dhurwa Zone forms a transition between the backward Dandami Maria on the southwest and the relatively advanced Muria tribal region on the northeast as marked by the local dress and houses. They are highly skilled basket weavers. Etymologically, Dhurwa means headman of the village. They are divided into number of exogamous and totemistic bansh or clan such as Bagh [tiger, nag [snake], Dokda [goat], Kachim [tortoise] etc.

Among them mangni or marriage by negotiation is preferred. Among other types of acquiring mates' marriage by elopment, junior levirate, junior sororate are common. Monogamy is the rule. System of bride price is prevalent.

Dhurwa settlement and villages are found mainly in the forest and it's neighbouring area of Darha ghat where plenty of bamboo groves are found. Since they are basket makers, they collect the raw materials like bamboo from their immediate niche. Along with this they also practise settled cultivation. They collect honey, resin, seeds, barks etc. from forest and sell those in weekly market. They have their own traditional council for social control headed by a Patel and assisted by Kotwar and an Aut Paharia. The post Patel is hereditary. Danteshwari mata is their principal deity. Other deities are Maoli Mata, Telgu Mata, Jalni Mata, Pitore Deo, Dongar deo, Hinglagin Mata etc. Their religious heads are Pelac and Pujari whose posts are hereditary.

BHATRA

The Bhatra tribe is settled in a small area of Indrawati plain in northern Jagdalpur, that is, the Bakawand circle. Beyond the district they are also found in Koraput district of Orissa. It is reported that they came to Bastar with the first Raja of Bastar from the Warangal. They are divided into three social groups namely, Amnit Bhatra or Bade Bhatra, Sargimundi or Majhli Bhatra and Shan Bhatra or Pit Bhatra or Batamundi Masnimara. Among them Amnit hold the highest status, Pit-Bhatra hold the lowest status among them and are derogatively called as Muria Bhatra. On the basis of economic criteria these divisions are formed. Amnit Bhatra is mainly concentrated in Orissa. Each group has a number of exogamous, totemistic clan. They are monogamous, but polygyny is also permitted. They have a system of bride price. Cross-cousin marriage is allowed. Beside marriage by negotiation other ways of acquiring mate are wdalya [marriage by elopment], paisa mundin [intrusion], rajikhusi [love marriage], marriage by service and khilnwa dibar [marriage by inheritance]. Now a days they are mainly cultivators. They also collect from forest various kinds of edible roots, tubers, leaves and mushroom for their consumption. They have their own jati panchayat headed by a Naik who is assisted by Paik and five members.

Religiously, Bhatra are divided into two set viz., Jagatlok and Bhagatlok. The Jagatlok Bhatra practice their traditional religion while the Bhagatlok Bhatra are a group of converted Bhatra into Alekh Dharam, worship only one formless supreme authority called Alekh Mahaprabhu.

They wear saffron coloured cloth and are vegetarian. All the Bhatra pierce their ear lobe before marraiage but Jagatlok only wear sacred thread.

They depend much on supernatural power. They worshp their ancestors, their Gotiadeo, family deity etc. Danteshwari ma – the chief deity is believed as their protecting goddess. They also worship Bhima deo, Maoli mata. They also have faith in *panghin* (witch) and a *sirha* can practise witchcraft in the form of *ban mara* (lamprey) that is, to do some harm to any person with the help of his supernatural power through his deity.

HALBA

The Halba tribe lives in small scattered area in many villages of north and south Bastar, on old administrative centre of the Bastar State like Bijapur where Halba men were posted as sepoys. In M.P. they are numerically dominant community in Bastar and Chhattisgarh area. The origin of the name of Halba is derived from hal [plough]. The Halba of M.P. claim superior status over Ghasi, Mahara, Maria, Gadaba etc. and are divided into two endogamous and territorial divisions viz. the chhattisgarhia and the Bastaria. Again the Bastaria Halba are divided into two endogamous division – (i) Purit or Jat Halba and (ii) Surit or Nani Halba. The Purit claim superior status over other. Each of these divisions again is divided into number of exogamous bans [clans] such as Nag, Bhagel, Netam, Kashyam, Kachim etc. Marriage by negotiation is common but marriage by elopment [pisamundi], marriage by service occur frequently.

They are agriculturist. They have their own mechanism of social control. The principal deity is Danteshwari mai. Along with this, they also worship several deities like Maoli, Bhairam, Jhangda, Mahamai and several village deities. They also practice ancestor worship. Their eldest clan members in the village perform their own rituals.

From the above discussion it reveals that different tribal groups of Bastar occupy a specific territory in which they practice all their socio-cultural behaviour and maintain their identity. If we consider the social organization of the above mentioned tribal groups it is found that more-or-less their social structure are the same i.e. they have system of phratry, which is exogamous and totemistic. Due to territorial difference their name may be different. All are believers of ancestor worship, soul worship and have faith in spirits. In most of the cases they try to appease the deity, which again depend on their natural environment and resources, for the welfare of family and community. It appears that inspite of micro level differences in their social organization, they perhaps belong to the same stocks, who are settled in different corners and territory of district – Bastar and in course of time and through the process of acculturation they form an endogamous group.

In Bastar there are at least seven major tribal groups who are settled in various corners of the district and maintain their individual cultural identity.

Chapter-4

Religious Belief: Rituals and Festivals at Pargana or Village Level

Life in India is a mosaic of colourful happenings. The festivals are not mere occasions but deep-rooted traditions and customs woven into the fabric of Indian life. One of the most important outward manifestations of religion is the performance of festivals and it has been an important feature of group life all over the world. Festivals are woven into our cultural fabric. All of them brighten the Indian landscape and add to the variety and spice of our life. Each one of these festivals has its own distinguishing features but taken together they have an underlying rhythm and tenor, which signifies Indianness (Singh, 1982).

Religion cannot be seen but is only felt through empathy. Outward manifestation of religion comes through its active part that is through the performance of rituals and festivals. These are the ways to propitiate and show honour to the supreme authority to appease him for blessing. A person gets mental strength out of it. Ritual is the process of propitiation of deities (Sarkar and Dasgupta, 1996).

India being a multi-ethnic country with heterogeneous culture having various religious faiths, which are respected as well as honoured by all the ethnic groups. In spite of possession of various religious stigma by ethnic groups, there are some occasions where some rituals and deities are equally respected/honoured by all the ethnic groups perhaps, chiefly due to their survival strategy.

Bastar being the study area is a region where people of various cultures live together, often sharing each other's culture traits. Through their sharing and borrowing of such traits of neighbouring communities, the people of Bastar representing a clear picture of cultural admixture especially admixture in religious pantheon

It also appears that there are three main categories of deities prevalent among the tribal of Bastar –

a) Earth goddess
b) Lineage deity and
c) Matagudi

Earth Goddess

In each and every village in Bastar all the ethnic groups propitiate these three categories of deities where ethnic boundary is not taken into consideration. It is reported from Tamakoni, Machkot, Nagarnar, Pandripani and Tiriya villages that earth is referred as *bhum* or *matideo* or *mutak* or *murtal* or *tallurmutte* or tallin. The earth includes the spirits of river, forest and appeased separately. In Tamakoni village these are appeased with the help of **Pujari** from Amnit Bhatra group while at Machkot it is officiated by Dhurwa priest or *perma.*

The tribal people of Bastar venerate the earth goddess in different names, which varies according to their territorial settlement pattern. Abujh Maria and Muria refer her as *tallurmutte*. **Tallin** by Dandami Maria, *mutak – murtal* by Dhurwa of Kanger ghati area and *bhum* or *mati deo* by Bhatra, Halba and neighbouring villages of Jagdalpur. They have also a belief that they are her offspring as she feeds them by providing various types of crops and cereals. The Hindus identify the earth deity as *matti deo/matideo*. It is worshipped in the lighter half of the month of Chait (March-April) and the ritual is officiated by a *gaita or sirha* of tribal origin or by a Mahara caste and referred as *matipujari* and it is performed in day time. They have a belief that *matideo* also gives protection to their cattle. They worship the *matideo* to protect the village from all types of diseases and dangers. It is observed that each and every village of Bastar including our studied villages has its own deity called *gaon devi* or *mata gudi*; in Tamakoni village **Maolimata** and **Jaliniburi mata** are presided in village *matagudi* while in Machkot village it is presided by **Maolimata, Pardeshin mata** and **Telangin mata**. They are worshipped for the welfare of the village. Beside all the deities the village under study has its guard deity who are usually established at the outskirts of the village. The deity exits as a guard deity and protects the village from all types of evils (Dasgupta and Sarkar, 2003). These deities are identified or **Dand deo**(male deity) in both the studied villages.

Lineage Diety

Ancestor worship is one of the essential parts in the life and action of the tribes of Bastar. They believe that their deceased ancestors are among their own household deities who protect them from all sorts of problems and act for their welfare. The ancestral spirit holds a very important position in their culture and religious world. All tribes of Bastar practice ancestor worship. It is also reported that Abujh Maria, Dandami Maria, Muria and Dorla have their own *pen* (clan) deities (Dasgupta and Sarkar, 2002). This *pen* deity is a guardian deity of a particular clan to which a person belongs. These entire *pen* deities of the celestial world are mythically connected with each other through the network of social relations; more so, these deities have their own specified territory. **Anga** is the blanket term for all the clan deities. Some of the *pen* deities are male and represented by a frame of three parallel log of *saja* wood or log held together by cross-pieces of bamboo to which they are tied by cords of *siyari* creeper or twisted thongs to the outer ring of bamboos (Grigson, 1991). When the *pen* deity is a female then it is represented through *lat* (which is a long bamboo stick with a piece of coloured cloth which indicate the flag of a particular deity and tied at the top and above that at the extreme end there is a small conical or round bell metal piece in which the *lat* is inserted). This is known as *gura*. The log gods are commonly known as *anga deo or pat deo*. The *pat deo* deity is propitiated by the communities living in and around Jagdalpur, Dantewada and Chote Dongar areas while *anga deo* is the deity of Muria tribe of Narayanpur area. It is also reported that each and every clan has its own log god and among the log gods there are some sorts of hierarchy (Sarkar & Dasgupata). To detect the culprit they usually take help of their own clan god (log god). In case of any crisis, problem in a house the even the non-tribal people of the village are inviting log god to visit their house and offer blessings. The clan god is carried on shoulder of four people from some other village. They carry it and take round in the village, visiting each and every household. The clan priest also accompanies the party. It appears that the carriers of the log god are possessed and their each and every act during such carrying procession is considered as the directives of their supreme authority of celestial world.

Matagudi

The site of a *mata gudi* is found in each and every village of Bastar. In a village *mata gudi* there are places for other various *matas*, which are related with family welfare activities. Some of such deities are **Pardeshin mata,**

Bhandarin mata, Sitala mata, Telangin maga, Jalini mata, Maolimata, Kankalin mata, Kodai mata, Jamindarin mata, Danteshwari mata, Mahamai ma, Hingala devi etc. of which **Danteshwari** (or **Yayal muttey**) being the supreme among them.

Annual Ritual Calendar

The empirical data has been collected chiefly from Tamakoni, Machkot, Nagarnar and Pandripani villages. The ethnic composition of the studied villages is as follows :

Ethnic composition of studied village

Name of the villages	*Ethnic groups*
1. Tamakoni	Bhatra (ST), Raja Muria (ST), Dhurwa (ST), Kurak/Dhimar.
2. Machkot	Dhurwa (ST), Raut
3. Nagarnar	Bhatra (ST), Kumhar, Sundi, Ghadwa, Panika, Mahara, Lohar Chandal
4. Pandripani	Halba (ST), Gond (ST), Muria (ST), Dhurwa (ST), Sonar Dhakar, Sundi, Khatri

In Bastar the people, both tribal and non-tribal, observe several rituals and festivals. Some rituals are performed at the family level, some at community level while rest at regional level. The empirical data also speak that they have a celestial world where a large number of deities are there and which are genealogical related and are propitiated by them. Numerous *devis* (mother goddess) are in their belief system for their various socio-economic welfare. Their celestial belief system is full of myth and legend and which are directly influencing their sustenance activity.

Annual Ritual Activities under Studied Villages

Category: (i) Earth Goddess (E); (ii) Lineage Deity (L), (iii) Matagudi (M)

Month	*Name of Village*	*Name of Deity / festival*	*Purpose*	*Place*	*Level of Worship*	*Officiated by*	*Category*
1. Chait (March-April)	Tamakoni, Machkot, Nagarnar & Pandripani	Maoli mata (or matti deo or bhum deo)	For welfare and especially to get good harvest. She is appeased first after that *bij putni* ritual is practiced in the next month. It is also a worship of earth	At village mata gudi	Village level	Tribal Priest / Pujari (Bhatra)	'M' and 'E'
2. Baisak (April- May)		Bijputni Bhima deo	It is associated with agricultural activities For good rain	Close to village Matagudi Courtyard of village priest	Family level Communal participation	Do Tribal priest	'E' 'E'
3. Landi (May – June)		Deogudi Bazar (Soshon pahin mata)	To save them from disease and dangers	Outskirt of village	Village level. Both Tribals and Hindus jointly perform this.	Do	'E' and 'M'

Month	*Name of Village*	*Name of Deity / festival*	*Purpose*	*Place*	*Level of Worship*	*Officiated by*	*Category*
					All the neighbouring deities are invited who attend the ritual with *chata* or *lathi*		
4.Goncha (June – July)		(a) Goncha (Cart festival	Welfare	Jagdalpur	Communal participation	Aryanak Brahma	'E'
		(b) Amush (or hariali)	Protect them from witches/ evil spirits roam in the air as well as cattle worship	At village individual houses	Family level	Family head	'E'
5. Amos (July – August)							
6. Bhado / Rassa (Aug. – Sept)	Tamakoni, Machkot, Nagarnar & Pandripani	Pola and Naya Khani / dhan noua	Harvested new paddy is offered to their ancestors	At individual house	Family level	Family head and village pujari	'E' and 'L'
7. Kuar (Sept. – Oct.)		Dusehra	Welfare	Jagdalpur	Communal participation	Brahmans	'M'

Month	*Name of Village*	*Name of Deity / festival*	*Purpose*	*Place*	*Level of Worship*	*Officiated by*	*Category*
8. Kartik (Oct – Nov)							
9. Aghan (Nov. – Dec.)		Lakshmi Jagar	For prosperity & fertility	Village *mata gudi*	By all tribal and Hindus	Tribal priest/ *perma* and sometimes along with Hindu priest	'M', 'L' and 'E'
10. Pus (Dec. – Jan)		Diari	Cattle worship	Individual houses	Family level	Family head	'E'
11. Magh (Jan – Feb)		Marai	Thanks giving ceremony to earth goddess	Collectively in one place of several neighbouring villages	Communal participation	Tribal priest **(Perma / Gaita)**	'E'
12.Fagun (Feb. – Mar)		Amanua / amakhani (sometimes it is performed in chait depends on *perma / pujari*	To offer new mango to their ancestor, only after this ritual they are allowed to eat mango	Village *mata gudi*	Communal participation	Tribal priest	'E' and 'C'
		Anga Deo/ Pat deo (clan deity)	Tribals worship their clan deities to show reverence to		Community level	Tribal of Bastar	'L'

Month	*Name of Village*	*Name of Deity / festival*	*Purpose*	*Place*	*Level of Worship*	*Officiated by*	*Category*
		He is worshipped in all rituals/ festivals	the deity from whom they have originated. Again both tribal and non-tribal take help of those deities to get protection from all evils and also to detect the presence of any evil eye.				

Apart from these there are number of **Mata** in the respective villages, which are also appeased time to time in order to get blessings and welfare for family. In the following lines we shall try to portray some of such **Mata** deity in the studied villages.

A. Tamakoni Village

(i) Jhanda Deo and Duarmundia

It is situated in the village boundary to protect the village from any kind of calamity and both these are male deity, officiated by Bhatra *pujari*. He is appeased through pujari where all the members of village participate and contribute. Stone and stick represent him.

(ii) Maolimata

She is worshipped for the welfare of village and cattle. She is worshipped at *mata gudi* of village by Bhatra priest (of Amnit Bhatra group, wearing sacred thread) and represented by a piece of stone. She is especially appeased during Holi and failing which he or she would face bad things in the village, known as *dath parna*, she is also worshipped on every Saturday and Tuesday. She is regarded as Sister of Mata Danteshwari – the tutelary deity of Bastar king.

(iii) Jaliniburi mata

She is represented at village *matagudi* with unhewn stones, ritual officiated by village priest(from Bhatra community), she is appeased for Cholera, Pox, dysentery and vomiting etc and during Fagun (Feb-March) she is worshipped by all the villagers community especially on every Tuesday and Saturday of the week.

(iv) Dongar deo

He is also placed in the outskirt of the village. He is a male deity, appeased once in a year when buffalo sacrifice is done. The ritual is officiated by village Bhatra pujari for the protection of village from any external hazards.

(v) Dand deo

He is a male deity. He is appeased by village *sirha* (sorceror) who is from Raja Muria. He is a male- volent deity. He is appeased in order to save from malevolent spirit. All the villagers take part in this ritual.

B. MACHKOT VILLAGE

(i) Pardeshin mata

She is presided at village *matagudi*, represented by small terracotta icon. She is worshipped for welfare in family. Before eating any new seasonal fruits / cereals first she is appeased e.g., during *amakhani* ritual(first eating of mango in a season). On each Wednesday and Saturday she is worshipped by Dhurwa pujari / perma with incense and coconut. Apart from this she is worshipped with éclat during brighter half of the Chait month. She is also worshipped during *noakhani / nayakhani* in the month of *bhado* by village *sirha* (sorceror). All the villagers participate in it.

(ii) Telangin mata

She is very ferocious and angry deity, represented by thorny seat with iron nails in the village matagudi. Before harvesting of paddy she is appeased on behalf of village by Dhurwa *pujari / perma* by sacrificing egg at *matagudi*, which is known as *pit kutani*, only after paddy harvest is started by villagers. She protects from the evil eye during harvesting.

(iii) Bhairam devi

She is worshipped for the welfare of cattle and to save from fever and appeased by *sirha* of tiger or nag clan. Stone represents her.

(iv) Bhandarin mata

She is represented by a khuta of wood equivalent to horn of wild buffalo, officiated by *pujari* and rituals performed for a cluster of neighbouring villages for the welfare in family.

(v) Maoli mata

Represented by small terracotta icon, officiated by Dhurwa pujari, worshipped for welfare in family and cattle and also considered as sister of Danteshwari ma or Hinglajin mata. In Gondi she is called as *yagal muttey*.

(vi) Ganesh Puja

It is a recent induction in the village, officiated by Brahman priest of Jagadalpur in the month of Bhado. This puja continues for nine days where all the villagers subscribe for the ritual. During this puja loudspeaker with Hindi songs are played.

C. NAGARNAR VILLAGE

The village shrine or *matagudi* is presided by **Jalini Mata**, ***Pardeshin Mata*** who is chiefly worshipped during Fagun (Feb-Mar) and Landi (May-June) communally by village

Bhatra priest. There is also a *bhima khuta* (rain deity) in the village, which is also officiated by a Bhatra priest for good rain. This ritual is performed sometimes from Chait (March-April) to Landi (May-June). **Bhandarin Mata** and **Telangin Mata** are worshipped by Bhatra pujari during Kuar (Sept-Oct.). Unhewn stone represents all these deities. Another *Mata,* living goddess, named **Kankalin Mata** is appeased by a different Bhatra *pujari* during Magh (Jan-Feb). The purpose of this ritual is thanks giving ritual for good harvest. She is equally considered by them as **Danteshwari mata**. It is also communal ritual in the village where all the villagers voluntarily contribute for such ritual. Apart from this, a few households in the village practiced **Lakshmi Jagar** ritual during Pous (Dec-Jan), though it is individual family level worship but all the villagers participate in it. The priest is Brahman in this ritual. Case history reshowseals that this ritual is performed at Bhatra family last during 2002 in this village.

D. PANDRIPANI VILLAGE:

Some tribal households of this village, namely, Bhatra and Halba, have *tulsitala* (Basil plant) in the courtyard. According to the Hindu mythology *tulsi* is equivalent to Narayan and these tribal people (only male) wear *Kanthi* garland in the neck. Pujari is from Dhakar and Muria tribe of the village.

There are following *matas* in the village who are appeased time to time by *pujari* and where all the villagers both Hindu caste group and tribal jointly participate and perform their respective role for happiness and welfare of their village, cattle, crops and family.

At Hazariguda Para of the village there is a seat for *mata* who is especially appeased during Holi (i.e., in the month of Fagun) and Goncha (cart) festival by Muria *pujari* in order to save form pox. It is performed communally where all the villagers contribute. An anthropomorphic icon represents her.

At Maoliguda *para* of the village there is a place for *Maolimata* who is represented by unhewn stone. She is regularly appeased on Saturday and Tuesday by Dhakar priest. She is also considered as the sister of **Danteshwari mata**. During Holi in the month of Fagun (Feb-March) she is specially appeased communally by collecting contribution from the villagers, otherwise her wrath will harmful for the villagers.

The **Banshbhundi Mata** is situated on the entrance of main roadside, near *damor* factory and on the western outskirt of the village. Unhewn stone represents her. All the villagers communally perform her ritual by collecting contribution twice in a year and her ritual is officiated by Dhakar(cultivating caste) priest. First she is appeased during Goncha/ Ashar month in the lighter half for good rain and secondly, she is worshipped during the lighter half of the Pus (December-January) month for the welfare of their cattle and on the same day they also perform **Diari** festival of the village. Along with this ritual on the same day at Karehkote para of the village Boriyadi Mata is appeased communally which is also officiated by Dhakar priest. She is also represented by unhewn stone.

They also appeased **Hinghlaji Mata** communally for peace and welfare of the village during Fagun (Feb-Mar). It is continued for three days and officiated by both Muria (ST) and Dhakar pujari of the village. Pig, cock and goat are offered in this ritual for sacrifice. Muria(ST) sacrifices pig while goat is sacrificed by Halba (ST). During this ritual all the neighbouring village deities are invited since all these **Matas** are genealogically related in their celestial world.

They also perform worship of **Bhima- Bhimul Khutha** for good rain by the Muria (ST) tribe communally in the village. She is appeased by *pujari* twice in a year that is during Holi in the month of Fagun and during Goncha (cart) festival in the month of Goncha (June-July). The seat of this benevolent deity is at Hazariguda para of the village.

Besides these, in each and every shrine of village *matagudi* there is an open space for **Dand deo**, whose wrath is harmful for village welfare. He is also appeased with the help of *pujari* of the village.

The villagers also have faith and perform **Lakshmi Jagar** in the month of Aghan to Pus (Nove-January). This ritual is continued for a month and officiated by Muria (ST) and Dhakar priest. Though it is performed at family level but all the villagers participate and take active part. Once this ritual is performed in the family, it is then obligatory for such family to perform the same ritual for two consecutive to years. This ritual is a symbol of prosperity among them and widely accepted by both Hindu and tribal neighbours of the village.

The seat of **Pardeshin Mata** is also at Hazariguda para along with **Mata.** She is specially worshiped during harvesting, *amakhani* and *nayakhani* ritual by Muria (ST) *pujari.*

Conglomeration of Mata Cult Network and Impact

There are mainly two kinds of religious organizations found in human societies. In primitive and archaic societies, religion is a different phenomenon; many forms of human association from the family to the work group, have in some important respects a religious character. In these societies, religion is one aspect of the life of all social groups. However, religious and magical specialists appear early in societal development and religious individualism may be found in contemporary non-literate societies (o'dea, 1969).

Religious institutions evolve as patterns of worship, that is, as cult; they evolve at the same time as patterns of ideas and definitions, that is, as beliefs; and they emerge as forms of association or organization. The cult has a mysterious value, which is attached to it that we cannot fully rationalize

(Mead, 1934, p.296). The relationships acted out in the cult are first of all relationships with the sacred object.

In each and every villages of Bastar there are a number of *matas(*or a kind of Mother goddess cult) who are appeased from time to time for welfare and blessings, otherwise their wrath may lead a troublesome life. The seats of these *matas* are in village shrine and some of those *matas* are already discussed in the preceding pages. Incidentally these *matas* are genealogically related to each other in their celestial belief system that again have some consanguineal or affinal relations with the supreme deity of Bastar – the **Danteshwari mata**, the tutelary deity of Bastar king/ royal family.

The whole concept of various *matas* or mother cults as found in different villages of Bastar centers around the principle mother cult, **Danteshwari**, which acts as a centripetal force. During **Dusehra** festival we have observed the centripetal nature of the worship of the mother cult since all the individual village deities are brought in to Jagadalpur town for propitiation centering around **Danteshwari mata**. The forces of decentralization of all these individual deities take place soon after the **Dusehra** festival when these individual deities return to their respective villages after performing *bidai* or *gangamunda yatra* ritual at Gangamunda ward of Jagadalpur town.

The whole idea of centripetal nature of religious beliefs percolates in all strata of the society where the tribal and non-tribal ways of life form a bond of synthesis, at least in their religious world-view and socio-economic understanding of life. This impact is strongly evident in the life and culture of the people of Bastar at large even to this day though it might have crystallized during the reign of feudatory chiefs, who ruled Bastar till recent past.

Chapter– 5

Bastar Dusehra Festival – The Process of Assimilation and Integration

Bastar Dusshera is something unique. It is one of the chief festivals of Bastar, originally patronized by Royal family. The most important of these in Bastar is the Dusshera when all local deities from all Parganas and villages are invited and congregate at the temple premises of Danteshwari in Jagdalpur – the district headquarter. The Dusshera in Bastar, unlike Dusshera in other parts of India, has nothing to do with the triumphant return of Rama to Ayodhya. Dusshera in Bastar is devoted entirely to the goddess – **Devi Danteshwari**. Bastar Dusshera has several components and each of which has a history of its own in which specific division of labour among the various ethnic groups of the district or subalterns of the state is highly marked. Dusshera in Bastar is an occasion to propitiate the supreme goddess – **'Danteshwari mata'** of the local pantheon. It is also reported from old inhabitants of Jagdalpur town that in early days during the regime of Late, Pravir Chandra Bhanjdeo, on the eve of this occasion, the village / *pargana* headman and other office bearers and the feudal chiefs, the local diviners, shamans, priests (*pujari* or *gaita*), sorceror (*wadde)* etc. used to attend the function at

Jagdalpur along with the respective village deities (i.e., either carrying the umbrella or *chhata* or *lathi* of the deities), carried in litters. Tribals from distant villages used to stay in the neighbouring forested area and within the open space of the town during these festival days, which continues for about 15 days.

It is also reported that Dusshera and circumambulation of *rath* or chariot was started during the regime of **Raja Purushottam Deo** –king of Bastar **during 1468 – 1534**. The Dusshera intricately inter related with number of villages and *parganas* with various ethnic groups. In Bastar Dusshera, this festival is usually started on the day of *kumb* or new moon of the month Saon (July-Aug.). On the same day the villagers also perform **Amush** or **Hariali**. From that day they start to bring wood for the construction of eight / four wheeled *rath*. On that day they worship the *pata* wood (the main support of chariot) before Danteshwari temple. The construction of base of chariot is initiated by ritual **magar muhi** when wooden support is provided to the base. Blacksmith of Pandripani and Tekamera villages and Agarias does the fixing of wooden joints with iron nails. Before construction of chariot they perform a ritual – **barsi utarni** when they worship the tools and equipments used for construction of the chariot. A goat is sacrificed and liquor, bangles, camphor, incense sticks, coconut are offered. After the construction of chariot wheels is over and before the holes are perforated **nar phodani** ritual is performed and offerings are alike with **barsi utarni**.

There is an intricate division of labour in making *rath.* **Raini rath** (or vijay rath) is eight wheeled while the **phool rath** is the smaller or four-wheeled chariot. The overall responsibility of the construction of chariot is traditionally vested upon the "Savara Naiks" of the village 'Bera umargaon' and 'Jhar umargaon' of Bakawand block of Jagdalpur. The ethnic groups involved in this construction work are Bhatra (ST), Saora (ST) and Raut; and they are altogether 177 in number and Dalpati Naik is *mukhia* of this group who hails from Saora community. It is also reported that there are a few Agaria who are traditionally iron smelters and provides nails for this work and Bhatra and Dhurwa are engaged in making rope for pulling the *rath*. The wood for various parts of *rath* is supplied from various villages of Bastar and it is estimated in this work about 75-80 villages as well as villagers are directly involved. There are some important pieces of wood used in *rath* construction, namely *pata wood, magar muhi, acchanda diwas, gola_sarai, kaichi_*wood – cross beam (for support), *khamba* wood (wood from base to top), *dhaman* wood (for *rath* top*), kami sarai, tarla patta*(for roof purpose), and *parla whokana*. It is also observed that the size of **raini-rath** is about 30 to 32 feet long, 18 feet wide and 18 feet height while the size of **phool rath** is about 32 feet long, 17 feet wide and 17 feet height.

It has been also observed that only one chariot is constructed yearly. In one year they construct the **raini rath** and the next year they construct the **phool rath**. After the chariot is constructed, the villagers of Mograpal decorate the chariot and it is known as **rath singarni**. At the beginning of the movement of chariot they perform a ritual – **rath-rengani**.

Next phase of the ritual is to take permission from **Kachan Devi** to celebrate Dusshera festival. It is a swing in the **'kachan gudi'** – the abode of the deity at Pathraguda of Jagdalpur town. The seat of the swing is made of thorns of '*bel*' tree. They perform the ritual on the new moon day of the month Aswin(Sept.-oct) i.e. on the day of *pitrapaksha* or *mahalaya.* on this day both **kachan devi** and **raila devi** are appeased – the most revered deities of both Panika (weaver) and Mahara (untouchable caste) communities. They believe that **Kachan devi** protects their wealth. As per their legend Kachan devi and Raila devi are two sisters and Raila is young, who married outside in a community of lowerrung in hierarchic ladder and thus was refused by her family as a daughter. Perhaps during that time Mahara and Mirgan accept her as their deity when her elder sister is also worshipped. In fact with the blessing of Kachan devi Raja Vir Narayan Deo's(1639 – 54) wife gave birth to a daughter. The **Kachan gudi** ritual is officiated by Panika priest since time immemorial while the priest of "Raila Devi" belongs to Mirgan jati – Harijan community. On this occasion they select a virgin of Panika caste who becomes possessed by the deity – **Kachan**. The duty of virgin girl is performed by Kunti Baghel, Panika Caste, Age – 8 and student of class-IV; for the previous 4 days she perform fasting. The priest hails from Manikpuri Panika caste of Rajen ward, Jagdalpur. On this occasion '**gurumaya**' – the two women of Panika caste play on *dhanku* – a musical instrument (a bow with string) to invoke the deities. The virgin becomes possessed and moves round the swing for three times along with sorcerer and **Bhairam dev** and then she is seated on the swing and gives permission to celebrate Dusshera festival. Previosly Raja used to come to take such permission. Now the same tradition is also followed and present Raja accompanied by chief priest – Laloo Pujari and other dignitaries of *raj_paribar* and their journey route is cleared all sorts of malevolent spirits by **Anga_deoi** often it is also known as **Pat deo;** who is carried on the shoulder of four persons who are at that time possessed. They are also panika and Dhakar caste.

Next day after **Kachan gudi** that is, on the first day of the lighter half of the_month Aswin (Sept-Oct) they perform the ritual **Kalash Sthapana** or placing of brass tumbler in the interior of temple premises of **Danteshwari mata** filled with paddy grain. On this event 36 figurines of **Durga Devi** is made of silver, one nail like structure made of gold and the materials of offerings are given to the priest to start the ceremony. Twenty-eight Brahman priests are invited to perform the rituals associated with *kalash sthapana*. Fourteen of them recite the holy book Chandi and the other fourteen recite Saptapadi. It continues throughout the days and nights of *Navaratri.*

In the evening of the same day **Jogi bithai** ceremony is performed at Sirasar Chawk Bhawan – adjacent to the Palace of Jagadalpur town. According to myth when the king – Annam Deo left Warangal for Bastar, the Jogi of Halba community followed him and behind them **Mata Danteshari** also came. As per the dictum of the king one married man from Jogi of Halba caste keeps *sanjam* during Dusshera for remaining 7 days at a stretch. There is a pit in Sirasar Bhawan. The Jogi sits in the pit in prescribed posture. All these days he keeps fast on behalf of Royal family and takes only small quantity of milk. At the time of "**uthai**" or end of ritual, they are given cash along with goat, liquor etc. During present field investigation Jogi came from Bade Amabal village. On that day from the temple premises of palace Jogi comes with procession of *manjhi*(red turban),___*chalki*(red turban), *member manjhi*(blue turban), *munda baja* (beating of small drums by Munda community) along with the chief priest. Before coming to Sirasar Bhawan, he visits **Maoli/Mavli mata** temple for blessings. A Kalash or brass tumbler and sword of the king are kept beside Jogi. The rituals are performed throughout the day and on the 9th day and on the day of Mavli_Parghav the Jogi breaks his *sanjam* (self-restraint) and leaves his seat from the pit.

On the next day after **Jogi bithai** ritual the *phool rath* is drawn and during this period *navaratri puja* is performed every day for nine days. After the holy recital by the priest in the **Danteshwari** temple at Jagdalpur and placed on the *phool rath*. Then the chariot is drawn from Sirasar Chowk in a procession to take round of **Mavli Mandir** (considered as sister of **Danteshwari mata** and infact she is the tutelary deity of Royal family; it is reported that when Annam Deo fled from Warangal, he fled along with their tutelary deity whose position in Bastar is considered as sister of **Danteshwari mata**) in circumambulation and finally up to the **Singh Dyodhi** of **Danteshawri** temple. During circumambulation some persons continuously keep fanning the deity with *chavar/chamar* (whisk). The *rath* is drawn for five days and about 800-1000 villagers of about 30-35 neighbouring villages are assigned to pull the *rath* during these days (Sarkar and Dasgupta, 1996).

On the fourth day of the lighter half of the month Aswin (Sept-Oct) the **magarmuhi charani** itual is performed. After the completion of construction of new *rath* (chariot) when new wooden wheels are inserted, this ritual is performed with the sacrifice of a goat and two hens and labourers engaged in this work are from Bera Umargaon and Jharumargaon of Bakawand block which has already mentioned earlier. This ritual is important because in this ritual rope is tied for pulling the *rath* for circumambulation.

Next important ritual is **Nisha Yatra**. It is performed on the 8th midnight of *Navaratri*'. During the night at about 11.30 p.m. to 12 midnight they perform **Nisha Yatra** (*nisha* means night and *yatra* means sacrifice). On this event they prepare rice, pulses and milk porridge at the Mavli mandir and at midnight those are carried in earthen vessel by Dhakar, Halba (ST) and Bhatra(ST) in procession to **Khemeshwar devi** temple followed by Bhatra men carrying the earthen lamps known as *mal diya* lighted by oil of the bark of *char* tree. The lamp bearers carrying the lamps on their shoulders that are arranged in a series of wooden frame. At the **Khemeshwar devi** temple *bhog* ceremony is performed by present Raja, Raj Guru and chief priest and goats are sacrificed by *pharsa* (*tang*i or axe). Raja Muria (ST), known as *jalal* of Bhatpal village, does sacrifices the goat. This ritual is performed to appease their ancestors and **Khemeshwar** temple is regarded as village guard deity.

After the ritual at **Khemeshar** temple is over the procession returns bck to **Mavli** temple and goats are also sacrificed there. There after goats are also sacrificed at **Danteshwari** Mandir. In **Danteshwari** temple a pumpkin is also offered now, which is a symbolic offering just as buffalo was sacrificed in older days.

On the 9th day they perform **Kumari puja** in the Danteshwari temple. On this occasion nine virgins and one bachelor all less than 10 years old are worshipped. They are given *saris* and *dhoti* respectively. The bachelor is regarded as **Bhairam deo**. He sits separately in front of the virgins(*Kumaris*). On the same day Jogi leaves his seat. This ritual is forerunner of **Mavli Parghav** (i.e. reception of **Danteshwari** of Dantewada) in the evening on this day. On this auspicious day the invited deities from various places of Bastar reach Jagadalpur. They are represented in the form of *doli* (palanquin), *lat* (stick) and *chatter* (umbrella) etc. of the deities are brought from the villages by the villagers. The main deities are **Danteshwari mata** of Chhote Dongar of Naryanpur and Bade Dongar of Naryanpur tehsil. These two are the special invitees on this occasion. Formal invitation are sent to them in the form of cash Rs.5.00 each and one goat each and coconut, camphor, incense, bangles, vermilion etc. The priest of the two deities along with their companions also come to Jagdalpur on the day of **Mavli Parghav** and participate in the ritual procession (Sarkar and Dasgupta, 1996). Beside this, other gods and deities of various villages and *parganas* also participate. They are **Chepra guddan Mata** from Asana village, **Mavli Mata** from Madpal village, **Chorni Mata** from Morath Pal village**, Shitala Mata** from KankaPal, **Pardeshin Mata** from NengaRas, **Badi Mata** from Nalpawand, **Ganga dei** from Parwa, **Hingla Dei Mata** from Bakawand etc.

In the evening of 9th day of *Navaratri* or *nabami* the **Mavli Parghav** ritual is held. On the first day of *navaratri* the Rajguru sends invitation through a *majhi* to **Danteshwari** of Dantewada. Invitation is sent with Rs.101=00, a piece of towel, cloth, one cocoanut, incense, camphor, bangles, hair pins, bindi and red *tikli* (used in the forehead by a Hindu married girl) as a mark of homage to her. After that on the 9th day the palanquin and *chhatra* of **Danteshwari mata** of Dantewada along with some ornaments are brought to Jagdalpur with procession and are placed at **'Jiya Dera'**. The *chhatra* of Jagdalpur of **Danteshwari mata** is also brought to *jiya dera* and placed there in the company of *chhatra* of **Danteshwari** of Dantewada. Earlier the Raja of Bastar used to go to receive the palanquin and *chhatra* of **Danteshwari** on this occasion. Now Rajguru, chief priest receives her along with District Administration. The people of Jagdalpur receive her in a big procession. They light lamps, burn cracker, dance, and play and sing songs. The Bison-Horn Maria or Dandami Maria come in groups with traditional attire and dance with the rhythm of *mandal* and *nagera.* After receiving the *chhata/chhatra*, the chief priest (an Aryanak Brahman) brings it to the temple of **Danteshwari Mata** at Jagadalpur. In temple a goat is sacrificed and *prasad* is distributed.

On the tenth day they perform **Bhitar Raini** when eight wheeled chariot – **Raini_Rath** is drawn. Since this chariot is moved for the first time on the tenth day the offerings are given before its movements and goats are sacrificed. During the afternoon the chief priest sits holding the *chhatra* (umbrella) of **Danteshwari** of Dantewada is ceremonially placed on the **Raini Rath**. Previously the king played this role. Offering of *mogra* fish is made before the start of the movement of *rath.* The **Raini Rath** is drawn by Dandami Maria of Kilepal village area and this practice is continuing since time immemorial. In **Bhitar Raini** the chariot is drawn from Sirasar Bhawan taken round the **Mavli mandir** in circumambulation like **Phool Rath** and is taken to '**Singh Dyodi'** (main gate of palace). At this place the *chhatra* is taken down from the *rath* and kept at **Danteshwari** temple of Jagdalpur. Then some rituals are performed before *rath* by some married women who sprinkle mustard seed and salt to protect it from evil eyes. On the same day at night the chariot – **Raini Rath** is ceremonially stolen by the Bhatras (ST) who brings it to Kumbharakot.

The main ritual of **Bahar Raini** is performed at Kumbharakot on the 11th day of Dusehra festival. All the invitee deities of various villages and *parganas* along with the villagers are assembled at Kumbharakot from early morning. On this day Raja used to partake the food at Kumbharakot prepared from newly harvested crop. This ritual known as **Nayakhani.** Now a day this ritual is attended by present Raja (**symbolically because he has no authority, power**, etc.) with Rajguru and chief priest. Some sacrifices (goat and pumpkin) are also made there. A thatched hut on the bamboo pole is prepared, it is almost closed with single circular opening known as **Rani Mancha**. It is learnt that in early days **Rani** (queen) witnessed all the ritual activities at Kumbharakot sated on this **Rani Mancha** through the circular opening and villagers of Karanpur are entrusted traditionally with the construction of **Rani Mancha**. Now-a-days construction of such hut is simply a ritual activity among them. On that day Dhakar and Panika communities worship **Kachan devi,** make goat sacrifice in view of protection from infectitious diseases. In the evening of the same day the *rath* is drawn back by Dandami Maria with a large procession where present Raja stands on a jeep under the ceremonial umbrella of his kingdom.

On the 12th day of the ceremony of **Kachan Yatra** is performed at *Kachangadi*. On this event goat, pig and cocks are sacrificed and the same virgin girl who was seated on the swing made of thorns of 'bel' tree is brought and given cash and new clothes. Thus the ceremony ends with a belief that with this ritualistic performance the girl becomes free from her possessed state.

On the evening of the 12th day the next event of Dusehra festival is **Muria Darbar** which is an annual feature of Dusehra function since 1906 (Sundar, 1997) at Sirasar Bhawan. It is told that "it was started with the intention of training the king in administration and what we would today call 'communication skills'. It is an occasion when the adivasis of Bastar are told of noble intention of the state, exhorted to conserve forests and engage in improved agricultural practices. It is a moment for the profession and rewarding of loyalty and even for the voicing of those minor notes of dissent that are permissible within the structures of official patronage". (Sundar, 1997).

During **Manjhi Darbar** or **Muria Darbar** where customarily the King sits on the dais with the *pargana manjhi* (headman of cluster of villages, hereditary post and wearing red turban with black coat), *Naik, Chalki*(he is assistant to *manjhi*, hereditary post, *Chalki* wears blue turban while *Naik* wears yellow turban and he is supposed to receive the *chata* or umbrella of Danteshwari of Dantewada), *Munda baja* (hereditary post of a community and wears pink turban) *Member/Memberin, Kotwar and Sarpanch, Patel, Mukhiya*(these posts are government post and are selected through election) etc. to discuss and solve their problem and their request was also taken care of. Now-a-days instead of King the dais is chaired by (during 2004 Dusehra) Chairman of Dusehra Committee, Minister and MLA of Chhattisgarh, Collector of Bastar district and Executive Officer of Panchayat (a woman). It is essentially an assembly of **Manjhi, Chalki** and **Member** where they are allowed freely to express their demand, problem of their area before this **Darbar**(assembly) where administrators and policy implementers are also present and it becomes a direct interaction with state officials. Due to the pressence of **Manjhi**, often this Darbar is known as **Manjhi Darbar.**

It has been observed during **Muria Darbar** on 25.10.2004 at 2.30 p.m. that **Manjhis** express their grievance and demand before district and state authority:

Case 1

Tulsiram Pujari, Age-56, **Manjhi** Chotedongar Pargana, Muria(ST), expresses about village roads, deforestation etc.

Case 2

Sadasiv Thakur, **Manjhi**, Hamirgarh Pargana, Age-55, Caste – Dhakar is demanding for Rs.1000/- per month being remuneration for carrying out the duty of **Manjhi**. Till date they have not received any such amount from administration. Chief Minister assured them through the officials of State on the dais that from now onwards State administration will incur Rs.500/- and Rs.300/- p.m. to **Manjhi** and **Chalki** respectively.

Case 3

Koram Kaunreya, Age-52, **Manjhi** Goalkunda Pargana of Bhopalpatnam, Dorla Gond (ST). He expresses about unemployment in the area and due to such young generation are inclined towards Naxalite activities.

Case 4

Lakhindar, Age-65, **Manjhi** Chitapur Pargana of Jagdalpur Tehsil, Bhatra (ST). He expresses that due to good yield in this year with the blessing of **Danteshwari mata** the strength of crowd is more and earlier it happened during 1965.

From the above discussion it clearly reveals that right from the days of Maharajas, the system of political organization in Bastar has been a very interesting one. The rulers, who were also the chief priest of the goddess **Danteshwari**, were regarded as the political heads. The hierarchical authority is as follows – Diwan, Pargana Manjhi, Panchayat, Manjhi-Mukhiya-Member and Memberin. At every level an official enjoys its authority and sustenance directly from the one above it (Das, 1974). Therefore, from the top of power structure – **Maharaja** to the village grass root level with the help of the institution of **Manjhi**, the political network and authority was well inter connected and firmly established which helped Maharaja to unite its subalterns who are from various ethnic groups.

On the 13th day they perform **Ganga Munda Yatra**. This is held in Ganga Munda tank of Jagdalpur. This ritual is also known as **Kutumba yatra**. All the invited gods and deities brought from various villages assemble at this place for collective farewell through community sacrifices of goat, pigeon, chicken, egg (fertilized) etc. With the performance of some ritual, they offer some money to the persons who have brought the invited deities and then the deities return to their respective villages.

On 15th day **Danteshwari** of Dantewada is given bid farewell and it is the final ritual of Dusehra function. Her palanquin, *chhatra* and escorts return to Dantewada. In her farewell she is offered rice, wheat, flour, pulses, sugar, jaggery, ghee, mustard oil, lamp oil, chilies, three saris with silver embroidery, coconut, dhoti, goat, incense, camphor, cash, vermilion, bangles, mirror, comb, ribbon, hair pin, shawls etc.

Thus, Dusehra is the ritual, which brings the tribal and non-tribal Hindus, irrespective of their caste/ethnic boundary and status, close to each other, and it binds all of them by a single thread (Sarkar and Dasgupta, 1996).

Associated Ritual Component of Bastar Dusehra and involvement of Ethnic groups/villages

Ritual Components	*Communities / villages involved*
(i) Barsi Utrani	Bhatra(ST), Saora(ST), Raut, Agaria
(ii) Nar Phodan	- do -
(iii) Rath Construction	- do -
(iv) For bringing of various pieces of wood for rath construction : (a) Pata wood	Name of the villages involved: Ulnar, Talnar, Chitaloor, Nangur, Billori, Madmoor, Nagarnar, Sadgud.
(b) Magar Muhi	Pandripani, Bade Marenga, Bade Morathpal, Lendra, Rajur Kurundi, Dhanaloor
(c) Acchanda Diwas (d) Gola Sarai	Khutapar, Baniagaon, Belgaon, Mejpadar, Dhanpunji, Chokawada, Maganpur, Bahmni, Amaguda, Jirgaon, Khumli, Markel, Kopaganda, Chote Kawali, Chilkuri, Bademurma, Jamawada, Keshapur, Phurapal, Magnar, Neganar, Badepara, Telegarapur,Alanar,Merawada, Parpa, Duganpal.
(e) Kaichi wood(cross beam)	Erikpal, Koyapana, Sendwa, Chingpal, Arshkot.

(f) Khamba wood (wood for base to top)	Bringpal, Dimrapal, Khumar Marenga, Kilepal, Mahakapal, Kaknar, Chindbahar, Koyanar
(g) Dhaman wood (for top of chariot)	Tondapal, Badebadam , Chizaukutti
(h) Kami Sarai	Keshloor, Badearapur, Rajkot, Netmoor, Telimarenga
(i) Tarla patta (for roof purpose)	Birasguda, Badebadam, Kolabada, Bade Kawali, Parati
(j) Parla whokana	Mavli Padar village.
(vi) Rath Singarni	Aryanak Brahman of orissa, Panera (Mali)
(vii) Rath Rengani	Aryanak Brahman, Dhakar, Bhatra (ST), Jogi.
(viii) Kachan Gadi /gudi	Panika, Dhakar, Aryanak Brahman along with Royal family. (It is also observed in this ritual that two aged women known as *gurumaya* play *dhankul* (a musical instrument which looks like a bow with a string). Dhankul symbolizes wealth; it is also played during Lakshmi Jagar ritual. This instrument may symbolize the end of bow and arrow era which is full of uncertainity and emergence of stable economic condition in view of practise of settled cultivation where food is secured.)
(ix) Raila Devi	Mahara, Mirgan, Aryanak Brahman along with Royal family.

(x) Kalash Sthapana	At the temple premises by 28 Brahmans
(xi) Jogi bithai	Jogi of Halba (ST) caste, Aryanak Brahman, Munda (ST), Manjhi-Chalki (Bhatra Dhakar, Murias Dandami Maria, Abujh Maria etc.), Member Manjhi (of Munda, Bhatra, Dhurwa etc.)
(xii) Navaratri Puja (a) Circumambulation of rath within town - for rath pulling	Brahman Chiefly Dandami Maria for pulling rath, mundebaja (Munda) and others.
(xiii) Magarmuhi Charani	Lohar, Agaria
(xiv) Nisha Yatra	Royal family, Brahman, Dhakar, Bhatra, Raja Muria, Halba and others
(xv) Kumari Puja and Mavli Parghav (reception of Danteshwari mata of Dantewada)	Brahmans, Royal family, Dandami Maria, Rajguru and District administration.
(xvi) Bhitar Raini	Brahman, Dandami Maria, Bhatra
(xvii) Bahar Raini	Raja, Rajguru, Brahman, Dandami Maria, Dhakar, Panika and villagers of Karanpur
(xviii) Kachan Yatra	Panika, Dhakar
(xix) Muria Darbar	Manjhi, Chalki, Member, Patel, District and State Administrator.
(xx) Kutumba Yatra/ Gange Munda Yatra	All the invited deities are given farewell with the help of Brahman, Sirha (sorceror) and leske (tribal priest)
(xxi) 'Bidai' (of Danteshwari mata)	Brahman, Dhakar, Dandami Maria

Table 20 : Contents of Dusshera Ritual – 2004

Days	*Date*	*Time*	*Ritual Activities*
1.	13.10..04	Evening	Kachan Gadi ritual
2.	14.10.04	Morning Evening	Kalash Sthapana Jogi Bithai
3-9.	15.10.04	Morning Evening	Navratri Puja Circumambulation of Phool Rath
10.	21.10.04	Morning Evening	Durga Asthami Nisha Yatra
11.	22.10.04	Morning Evening Night	Kumari Puja Jogi Uthai and Mavli Parghav
12.	23.10.04	Morning Evening	Bhitar Raini ritual Circumambulation of Raini Rath
13.	24.10.04	Morning Evening	Bahar Raini ritual at Kumbharakot After Nayakhani ritual at Kumbharakot, the Chariot is pulled back to palace.
14.	25.10.04	Morning Evening	Kachan Yatra Muria Darbar / Manjhi Darbar
15.	26.10.04	Morning Evening	Kutumba Yatra Farewell to invited village deities
16.	30.10.04	Morning	Farewell to Danteshwari of Dantewada

Table 21 : List of Invited Manjhi and Chalki during Bastar Dusehra – 2004*

Sl. No.	*Name of Pargana/ village*	*Name of Person*	*Ethnic group affiliation*
A1 : **Jagdalpur Tehsil : Manjhi**			
1.	Khitlabal	Lalit	Bhatra (ST)
2.	Borigaon Rankera	Mahadev Manjhi	Muria (ST)
3.	Upanpal, Amoraghati	Ramesh	Bhatra (ST)
4.	Kilepal	Kahurami Ganga	Dandami Maria (ST)
5.	Chitapur	Lachindar Manjhi	Dhakar
6.	Amabal	Banguram Chingru	Bhatra (ST)
7.	Godia	Balaram Banjhi	Muria (ST)
8.	Manjhiguda	Jhitak Manjhi	Bhatra (ST)
9.	Kesharpal	Mulchand Manjhi	Muria (ST)
10.	Karehkot	Manglu/ Gajak	Dhakar
11.	Pandripani	Trinath	Muria (ST)
A2 : **Jagdalpur Tehsil : Chalki**			
1.	??	Raghunath	Muria (ST)
2.	Pandanar	Sonsuram	Muria (ST)
3.	Badurbel	Dhanurju	Bhatra (ST)
4.	Seoni	Bablu Mahadev	Muria (ST)
5.	Agarbara	Chamra	Muria (ST)
6.	Bastana	Hando	Dandami Maria (ST)
7.	Amorah	Rameshwar	Bhatra (ST)
8.	Badhanpal	Lachindar	Muria (ST)
9.	Kesharpal	Suklu	Muria (ST)
B1 : **Dantewada Tehsil : Manjhi**			
12.	Pharashwal	Arjun Karma	Dandami Maria (ST)
13.	Kuakonda	Laxminath	Telenga

14.	Katekalyan	Laxma Kohorani	Dandami Maria (ST)
15.	Turparash	Rupchand Manjhi	Telenga
16.	Mosalnar	Arjun Manjhi	Dandami Maria (ST)
17.	Baralnar Handawada	Murra Manjhi	Dandami Maria (ST)

B2 : Dantewada Tehsil : Chalki

10.	Bareh Gudra	Bhonduram	Dandami Maria (ST)

C1 : **Bijapur Tehsil : Manjhi**

18.	Cherpal	Jetty Mangalam	Mahara
19.	Bidiya	Ablam Rama	Dandami Maria (ST)
20.	Albada	Metha Handa	Dandami Maria ST)
21.	Bhairamgarh	Etbari /Sukhenath	Telenga
22.	Murchkinar	Aglabh Pallichnadra	Mahara
23.	Gangalur	Hemla	Dandami Maria (ST)
24.	Phutkel	Dashar Narseya	Mahara
25.	Bijapur	Rama Singh	Mahara
26.	Elmidi	Dhurwa Sankareya	Mahara
27.	Lanka	Muhunda Bhima	Abujh Maria (ST)
28.	Chinna Kawali	Jagham palli	Dorla Gond (ST)
29.	Badera	Sahadev Mangalsai	Telenga
30.	Mingachal	Mihiyami Podiya	Dorla Gond (ST)
31.	Mangnar	Gurami Chaitu	Dorla Gond (ST)
32.	Mirsur	Bunem Bandu	Dorla Gond (ST)
33.	Mangapeta	Saimek Buchheya	Dandami Maria (ST)

C2 : **Bijapur Tehsil : Chalki**

11.	Kalhali	Okham Honda	Dandami Maria (ST)
13.	Thulthuli	Marhi Phagu	Abujh Maria (ST)

D : **Bhopal patnam : Manjhi**

34.	Gilgicha	Kesteya Raj	Dandami Maria (ST)
35.	Lingagiri	Punem Hiriya	Dandami Maria (ST)
36.	Chandur	Basam Rajanna	Telenge
37.	Lingagiri	Murla Gunda	Dorla (ST)
38.	Goalkunde	Koram Kaunreya	Dorla (ST)

E : **Konta Tehsil : Manjhi**

39.	Dubbatota	Sablabh Ganga	Dorla (ST)
40.	Baila dodra	Soyam Rama	Dorla (ST)
41.	Kistarm	Karka Koteya	Dorla (ST)
42.	Jagar gunda	Somrath Retnaiya	Dorla (ST)
43.	Nagarath	Hemla Hirma	Dandami Maria (ST)

F1 **: Sukma : Manjhi**

44.	Hamirgarh	Sadasiv Thakur	Dhakad
45.	Chipurpal	Sonadhar	Halba (ST)
46.	Korra	Sodi Hirma	Dandami Maria (ST)
47.	Kerlapal	Kuhurami Dula	Dandami Maria (ST)

F2 : **Sukma : Chalki**

13.	Chindgarh	Aasman (Father-Gangadhar)	Halba (ST)

G1 : **Kondagaon : Manjhi**

48	Korohobeda	Sridatru	Dandami Maria (ST)
49.	Konguda	Kripasankar	Muria (ST)
50.	Gadhsiliyari Kodobhat Keshkal	Dhaniram Manjhi	Dandami Maria (ST)
51.	Athgaon	Somnath	Dandami Maria (ST)
52.	Bhatva	Kaja	Dandami Maria (ST)
53.	Baragiree Bangoli	Raghu	Dandami Maria (ST)
54.	Majhimatbal	Dashmuram	Dandami Maria (ST)
55.	Alor	Gadoran	Muria (ST)
56.	Khetarwal	Dular Singh	Dandami Maria (ST)
57.	Sonowal	Budhram	Dandami Maria (ST)
58.	Palli	Durjan	Dandami Maria (ST)
59.	Satgaon	Dumaru	Dandami Maria (ST)

G2 : **Kondagaon : Chalki**

14.	Kachora Sonawal	Padamram	Muria(ST)
15.	Masauri	Mahanjuram	Muria(ST)
16.	Esalnar	Hiralal	Muria(ST)
17.	Randhna	Dalsam	Muria(ST)
18.	??	Lakhuram	Muria(ST)

H1 : **Narayanpur : Manjhi**

60.	Surehbahi	Birju (Father-Jhitka)	Muria (ST)
61.	Manegaon Kholpati	Bandru	Muria (ST)
62.	Edka	Rainu	Muria (ST)
63.	Baghbeda Benur	Manguram	Muria (ST)
64.	Karangpal	Bamey(Father-Gado)	Muria (ST)

65.	Chotedongar	Birju (Father-Miktulenga)	Muria (ST)
66.	Tekamata Khalpatti	Sonru	Abujh Maria (ST)
67.	Orcha	Tondu /Kuma	Abujh Maria (ST)
68.	Kiskonda	Balram	Muria (ST)
69.	Kokameta	Kemey	Abujh Maria (ST)
70.	Pakurkal	Sukla	Muria (ST)
71.	Kachhapal	Lemau	Muria (ST)
72.	Antagarh	Sukulram	Muria (ST)
73.	Kakhagaon	Pisener	Muria (ST)
74.	??	Khoriya	Muria (ST)
75.	Ghattakal	Chirmu	Abujh Maria (ST)
76.	Kokapar	Mangturam	Abujh Maria (ST)
77.	Doraktuta	Baju	Muria (ST)
78.	Salemta	Mehttar Ram	Muria(ST)
79.	Amabeda	Sudu	Muria (ST)

H2 : **Narayanpur : Chalki**

19.	??	Debaruram(Father-Banduram)	Muria (ST)
20.	Karkogoan	Budhram	Muria (ST)
21	??	Sukalu	Muria (ST)
22.	??	Kulsinh (Father-Lachminath)	Muria (ST)

* Source : O.P. Dhawai, Tehsildar, Jagdalpur(October,2004).

Therefore, it appears that altogether 79 Manjhi and 22 Chalki of different Pargana of Bastar were invited by local government authority to conduct the Dusehra function with pomp and éclat.

Chapter-6

Lakshmi Jagar—A Sanskritic Ritual

In the whole forest clad area of Bastar, Jagar is one of the famous rituals where mythological illustrations are narrated through various musical performances and Halba(ST) and Dhakar are the key performers. There are four types of *jagar*, namely, *ashtami jagar* during the month of *bhado* on the eve of Lord Krishna's birthday, *tija jagar* when *Siva puran* are recited, *bali jagar*-appeasement of rain deity and *Lakshmi jagar*-chiefly a post harvest ritual for rice goddess. The word *jagar* can be interpreted as 'wake'. But the ritual also has entertainment value.

In the month of *pand* or *aghan* (November-December) the villagers perform Lakshmi puja in their own house in all the Thursdays of the month. It is generally performed very early in the morning. In this ritual they offer flowers and fruits, coconut to the deity. They worship Lakshmi for prosperity of their family.

Except this sometimes Lakshmi puja is performed elaborately for nine days continuously. It is known as Lakshmi jagar. Both the tribals and non-tribals perform it. Lakshmi jagar is observed by the authors at the Chhapra guda of Asna village of Bastar where it was perfonned by Dhakar family at their own house and field during the month of *magh* (January-February). They have informed that sometimes the villagers perform it by an individual family and sometimes collectively. When they perform it collectively, they collect the contribution from the families who want to perform and participate the ritual. At that time, they erect a pandel in the village generally attached to the priest's house. They perform the puja there in the pandel establishing the deity. When a family performs it individually, the pandel is erected in an open space of the house, generally in the courtyard. The pandel is constructed by four wooden logs (sal wood of about 5'height), which are installed in the floor, which form a rectangular space. These are thatched with leaves and one side of that rectangle is screened with a piece of cloth. This is generally used at the back portion.

They observe this ritual for nine days and it is started on any Wednesday of the month. From that day they continuously worship her for nine days. They worship her by burning ghee lamp, offering coconut, banana, flowers, incense etc. Ghee lamp is burnt during day and night of those nine days. During those days woman sing songs, playing *dhankul,* and during nights the villagers dance and sing and enjoy the night. On the eighth day they go to the field to ask for Lakshmi Devi to marry her with Narayana and on the ninth day or last day they perform the ritual elaborately. That day is the main day of performance of the ritual.

It is observed that in the pandel they keep several photographs of Lakshmi, Narayana, Hanumanji etc. deities. They also keep a coconut symbolizing Lord Narayana. In front of them they keep a small pitcher made of some metal specially copper, filled with water. The mouth of the pitcher is closed with a betel leaf upon which a ghee lamp is enlightened. They keep two big earthen pitchers on both the sides of the small metal pitcher. The two pitchers are kept empty. The women, who come to visit the deity, offer her a quantity of rice grain that is kept in those *mitti ka ghara* or earthen pitchers. These two are closed separately with winnowing fan. They keep a quantity of vermilion, some China rose flower on those winnowing fans and there is a large bow upon each of the *kula* or winnowing fan. These bows are known as *dhankul*; these are the musical instruments and used when the women sing song during Lakshmi jagar. The *jagar* singer is known as *gurumai* and its main performer is called, as *pat gurumai* while her assistant is known as *cheli gurumai*. Ghee lamps are lighted in the place. There is a wooden partition wall that is found behind the photographs and in between the photographs and the screen at the back portion. In the space between the partition wall and the screen they keep two *mans* (bowl like structure which are made of wood) filled with paddy up to the level of its mouth. They put a piece of cloth on each the *man* covering the opening as lid. They keep those *man* with paddy on the first day of the ritual at that place very secretly hiding from others. They' do not even touch them during those nine days.

On the first day of the ritual they keep mud mixed with organic manure (cow dung) in some leaf bowls. They put somc paddy grains in it and everyday sprinkle water in those leaf cups or bowls. These seeds automatically germinate; seedlings come out of the seed. For nine days they observe how much seeds are germinated. They have a belief that if the seedlings, which are locally known as bhojli, come out in large number, they will then get bumper crop. On the ninth day they observe how much seedlings have come out of the seed to judge their future.

Those who perform Lakshmi jagar, have to perform it for three years. The first year they perform *mangni*. It is the custom of selection of a bride with final offer of marriage with their bridegroom. Next year, they perform *sadi* or marriage and during the last year they perform *gahana* or remarriage of a couple after the girl attains her puberty. It is completely a Hindu custom. It is found in the studied village that they have completed two years of Lakshmi jagar. It is the third year or the last year of the *gahana.*

On the eighth day that means one day before the performance of the ritual, they go to the field at about 3 p.m. to ask for the bride in the field and to finalize the marriage. It is just a formality, because *mangni* is perfonned already before two years. They go to the field with flattened rice, puffed rice. curd, peas etc., and eat those in the field.

On the ninth day they go to the field where they worship Lakshmi-Narayana. They arrange for their marriage in the field. A pandal is constructed in the field where they keep it's four sides open. It is also thatched with leaves. When the ritual is performed by the villagers collectively, then they arrange for the ritual at the priest's field while when it is perfonned by a family, then it is performed in the family's own field.

It has been observed that they gather there in the field at about 2 p.m. They go there with that coconut which symbolized Narayana. They collect some paddy stalk from the field; cover it with a white cloth. Similarly they cover the coconut, symbol of Narayana with another white cloth. At the base of the stalk they keep an empty earthen pitcher. The paddy stalk symbolizes Lakshmi Devi. The paddy stalk or Lakshmi Devi is hold by a married woman and the coconut or Narayana is held by a man who is her husband. When they reach to the pandal in the field the man and the woman sit side by side. They sit on *tanti* (the platform of small height made by the strips of bamboo). The woman sits on the left side of the man. The woman holds Lakshmi at her left side and the man keeps Narayana on his lap. Then the ritual starts. It is observed that at the beginning the priest officiates the ritual. The priest belongs to the local tribal people. In the studied Chhapraguda of Asna village the priest is from the Bhatra tribe. After the priest officiates the ritual, the *Sirha* of the village drives out all the evil spirits. Then the married women present there start putting oil, powdered rice grain, turmeric powder on that couple's forehead and also to Lakshmi-Narayana. It is known as *tikan*. They offer flower garlands, fruits, flowers, coconut etc., to them. Ghee lamp is lighted and incense is burnt. They offer both in kind and cash also to the deities to show their respect. The offerings made to Lakshmi are stored in the earthen pot at the base of the stalk. In this way the marriage ritual is completed. It is found that the married women play vital role in that marriage ceremony. They sing songs where they describe several stories of Lakshmi and Narayana; some among which will be discussed afterwards. The unmarried girls may be present there only but cannot touch the ritual objects. The widows are strictly prohibited to attend the ritual.

In case the ritual is performed collectively at the village the priest and his wife play the role of that couple who sit with symbolic Lakshmi and Narayana as their representatives. When *tikan* (putting of oil, turmeric and rice powder to Lakshmi, Narayana and to that married couple) is completed, they start for the pandal in the village to perform rest of the rituals. If there is any plain road, they generally bring the deities by *ratha* (chariot) but if the road is not smooth, they carry them in the hands or on shoulders. Before they start, sprinkling of water from a jar by mango leaves cleans the road. In the water they keep a piece of bark of mango tree, a quantity of milk is also added with the water. It is known as *kasa pani*. It is regarded as a very holy water. It is sprinkled by a man and behind him women go sprinkling rice powder on the road and after them the deities travel with a procession.

When they reach the pandal, in the village, they keep Lakshmi and Narayana together at the pandal. As per Hindu mythological legend Lakshmi Devi sits at the left side of Narayana. Similarly the couple also sits beside them. Then the married men and women offer them (the newly married couple) presentations. At the end of the ritual of marriage they offer presentations to the deities. The village deities and the deities from the neighbouring village are invited in the marriage celebration and they all attend the ritual both in the field and also in the village. The villagers take the consecrated food and spend whole of the night by singing, dancing and playing. Next day during daytime they go to river Indravati- adjacent to the village with that symbol of Lakshmi and its immersion takes place there in the river. They do not immerse Narayana and they keep him in the village temple. On that day they take the *bhojlis* and keep those upon their ears. It is known as *bhojli bhet ghat*. It is the symbol of friendship. If one puts *bhojli* on another's ear, they become ceremonial friends locally who are known as *bhojli saheli*. In this way they make ceremonial relationship.

When they return from the river, they open the *mans* to see whether the paddy in those *mans* have increased or not. If they are over flown or raised crossing the level and a quantity is spread on the floor then they think that it has increased and it signifies bumper crop for the next year. Then they keep those in the granary. When they perform it collectively, each and every family takes a handful of the grains from the *mans* and keep those in their own granary. They give all the presentations and cereals stored in two big earthen pitchers during those nine days to the women who sang songs of Lakshmi-Narayana throughout those days. In this way they celebrate Lakshmi jagar.

Lakshmi jagar may be performed during the month of *aghan* (November-December), *pus* (DecemberJanuary) and *magh* (January-February). Once Lakshmi jagar is celebrated, it must be celebrated for the consequent three years. The first year is known as *mangni*, second year is regarded, as the year of *sadi* and the third or the last year is the year of *gahana*.

They perform Lakshmi jagar for fertility and prosperity. They have a belief that one, who performs it, will get bumper crop in the field. Their lands will be very fertile and similarly their women will be fertile. On this occasion a fair is held in the village and during the night, they enjoy with local *Nat*-a dance drama, performed by the local artists, generally from the Bhatra- a tribal community.

Song : Oral epic (translated in English version):

Lakshmi jagar epic is classic narrative structure. It has some sections. Initially it started with story of the origin of the universe.

1. *"In the beginning there was no earth no sky no underworld, nothing. There was only water of ocean. A lotus flower arose from the ocean. Lord Vishnu was born from that lotus. A flood swept Lord Vishnu away Basut Nang –the snake, was there and rescued Him. Then from Lord Vishnu's navel, a lotus flower arose; Brahma, his brother, was born from that lotus flower.........."*

2. The story of Mengin :

Meng is monsoon rain. Mahalakshmi is rice and the twenty-one queens are the various millets and pulses. The logic of the story implies other equations such as Narayan with the sun, Mahadev (Siva) as one who spread seed etc.

"King Meng and Queen Mengin lived in Mengpur. They had a nine-story palace with a garden an orchard and a hedge. They passed their time in peace and happiness............"

3. Story of Mahalakshmi is betrothed to Narayan:

"Mahadev went to Narayan and said to him , get up O babu. Clean your teeth, bathe and eat your food. I will arrange your wedding with Mahalakshmi...... "

"Mahadev and Parbati then arranged the things for the engagement ritual, assembled the men and women of Kailaspur and went to Manjpur for the ritual.

As they arrived in Manjpur Queen Mengin saw them and got them water and a small stool. .... King Meng then asked them the purpose of their visit. 'We have come for the engagement ritual'... ' She is not just my daughter King Meng said.;she belongs to the three worlds, she belongs to the animals and birds, I alone cannot give her , I will seek permission from others'. Everyone agreed with this engagement ritual. Wine was offered to the earth goddess.........The oil ritual will be on the sixth day, the tying ritual on the seventh day, the feast will be on the eighth day and on the ninth day you will go home' Thus the most essential ritual will be on a Tuesday, the oil ritual on a Wednesday and the tying ritual will be on a Thursday.That will be the wedding of Narayan and Mahalakshmi........"

Discussion

The musical instrument of singer by *gurumai* are the accumulation of *dhankul*- a big hunting bow, bowstring (*jhikan dori*), a split bamboo comb for striking (*chirani kari*), an earthen pot (*ghumra handi*), a winnowing basket (*dhakan supa*) and a small stool (*maci*). The earthen pot is put on a stand made of straw and the mouth of the pot is covered with a winnowing basket to form a resonator. One end of the bow is put on top of the basket and the other end on the floor. The right hand side of the bow has a serrated edge and the singer sits on small stool with her left leg over the bow. Pat gurumai swishes the serrated edge of the bow with the bamboo comb to produce rough grating sound. At the same time, she plucks the bowstring with her left hand on the first and third beat. The result is a regular loud-soft beat. (Gregory and Vaishnav, 2003).

Thus from the aforesaid data it can be said that in the ritual part there are *dhankul* (big bow with string), winnowing basket or *supa, bhojli* or paddy seedlings etc. and after analyzing their *jagar* songs it is seen that when they step into agricultural operation and influenced by dominant Hindu culture, they try to appease Lakshmi - the goddess of wealth and also appease their equipment like bow through which their early ancestors maintained their sustenance. Truly speaking the Dhakar/ Dhakad community of Bastar is the peasant community from foraging hunter-gatherer stage to agricultural stage; their clans are totemic in nature. The worldview also speaks for development of human society from early days where great Hindu myth, riddles are also incorporated into their way of life. It is a thank giving ritual after harvest of paddy by especially Halbi speaking agricultural group of Bastar. To our mind this ritual signifies a salute to bow and arrow era and also an appeasement to rice goddess-Lakshmi, the deity of wealth and prosperity, which means a stage from uncertainty to the entry of a stage of certainty. It is also observed that many Sanskritic tenets have been incorporated as a trait of this ritual.

Chapter-7

Process of Social Movement

The tribal societies in south-eastern part of Central India have long been in contact with non tribal population in various aspects of their life. With the passage of time there is a slow process of mobility, which often provides them a place in the Hindu fold (Sarkar, 1986). Involvement of the tribal group in such a slow process of social mobility and their subsequent merger into non-tribal societies, particularly in the Hindu fold in Central India were also observed by many earlier scholars like Risley (1969), Russell and Hiralal (1916), Bose (1941), Srinivas (1952, 1962), Sinha (1962, 1980) etc.

According to Risley (1969) "tribes are gradually and intensibly being transformed into castes". He also envisaged several distinct process of social mobility in this country, namely.

1. efforts of leading men of a tribe to enter into caste fold.
2. acceptance of certain religious faiths of a particular Hindu sect.
3. enrolment of a tribe or a large section of it in the ranks of Hinduism.
4. gradual conversion of a tribe or a large section of it to Hinduism without losing their tribal identity.

The Anthropological Survey of India identified a number of social movements (Singh, 1983), which can be broadly identified as--

a. Movement for political autonomy,
b. Agrarian and forest-based movements,
c. Sanskritisation processes and
d. Cultural Movement based on script and language (eg. bhagat movements in various parts of tribal infested area of the country).

A number of religious as well as reformative movements have developed among some tribal groups of central India, especially in the areas which once were ruled by small feudatory King, Bhagat movement of Bastar through Baba Bihari Das, one of such movement in the early 1970's, suggests that they had their starting point in the historical culture contact situations which made tribal cultures susceptible to the preaching of Bhagat leaders. And when a movement originates, it rapidly, draws the large-scale participation of the tribals desirous of moving upwards to gain a respectable social position by following simple Bhagat prescriptions. Such Bhagat communities developed an interest in puritanic ways of life and drew closer to Hindu society (Bhatt, 1983). From earlier studies it clearly reveals that the Bhatra tribe of Bastar took an active part in such movement. The Bhatra are semi-Hinduized since they have historical and prolong contact with the Hindus as thethen Maharaja of Bastar allotted land to the immigrant Hindu in the tract of Bhatra. The Bhagat movement promised the Bhatra a higher social rank.

The chief criteria of acceptance of such Bhagat movement of Bastar were as follows:

1. one who accepted a k*anthi* (a bead made of tulsi wood) from Baba had to pay a nominal charge of 0.25 paise became the follower.

2. to plant *Tulsi* (basil plant) and *bat* (banyan tree) in the courtyard of house and worship the plant every morning after taking a bath.
3. to sing Bhajan in praise of Ram every morning and evening
4. to give up eating of meat, mutton and liquor especially English liquor or wine. Rice beer and *Sulphi* (Sago plam juice) were not prohibited.
5. to give up the worship of any other deity except Ram.
6. to abjure all magical practices.
7. to avoid pre marital and extra marital relation.
8. to avoid adultery and rape.
9. to abstain from violence, theft and telling lies.
10. to avoid eating or drinking water from persons who did not wear a *Kanthi.*
11. Married women were asked to put *sindur* or vermilion in the forehead.
12. to maintain cleanliness throughout the day.
13. to organize a bhajan in the village at least once a week or on market day.

All these were to introduce the ideal behaviour pattern based on puritanism in the life of the tribal and eliminate impure elements from it.

Under this backdrop a profile of Bhatra religiosity at Bastar is being discussed in order to understand the social stratification within the endogamous ethnic group. A kind of social mobility among the Bhatra clearly suggests for elevating the social position in society and creating distances through acceptance of some cultural traits of the caste Hindus (Sarkar, 1986).

II

The Bhatra are confined in small area of Indrawati plain in northern Jagdalpur, that is, Bakawand area and are divided into three main divisions viz, Bade Bhatra, Majhli Bhatra and San Bhatra. The details of such divisions are already discussed earlier in chapter-3.

So far their religion is concerned the Bhatra are divided into two groups, namely, *Jagatlok* – who are practicing traditional religions belief system, and *Bhagatlok* who are converted into Alekh Dharma, wear saffron coloured cloth, eat vegetarian food and lead a simple life.

Jagatlok

The Bhatra feel that the behaviour of the gods and goddesses are same as that of the men and women. According to Bhatra informants of Bakwand and Karpawand only difference between them is that the "gods and goddesses are having extra-ordinary power and cannot be seen but you can feel his or her existence". These gods and goddesses are often represented by stones. The *duma* (soul) of some legendary *sirha* (priest) who had extra-ordinary power has also been included into their pantheon. Their gods and goddesses are genealogically related in their celestial world and with the Danteshwari Mata-- the tutelary deity of Bastar King. Often their village gods and goddesses are invited in other village/ or villages through the dream of *sirha* where their agnatic kins of celestial world are living. A god or a goddess can inform the villagers of his/her presence through certain malevolent act and then communicate his/her desire through the voice of *Sirha*. When men and cattle of any village suffer frequently, then *sirha* is asked to find out the reason. Through trance *sirha* informs the desire of god or goddess to the village elders.

It has been observed that in each and every village of Bastar, there are number of *matas*, like, Bouriya mata, Telangin mata, Jalini mata, Sandei mata etc. Villagers of Bakawand are of the opinion that *mata* is very powerful deity and according to them there are about more than twenty sisters of *mata* who are distributed in various villages. The name of such *matas* are as follows :

i) Lanmi mata
ii) Lati mata
iii) Bouriya mata
iv) Pardeshin mata
v) Jatinbairi mata
vi) Bouri mata
vii) Sandei mata
viii) Mahamai
ix) Yogini mata
x) Kankalin mata
xi) Mangairini mata
xii) Telengin mata
xiii) Gharjamini mata
xiv) Takkakarin mata
xv) Hinghlaji mata
xvi) Banjarin mata
xvii) Pendra undin
xviii) Maoli mata etc.

And all the above *mata* have either consanguineal or affinal relation with Danteshwari mata—the chief goddess of Bastar, since it is the tutelary deity of Bastar Raja. It is believed that all the gods and goddess are originated from *mata*. In some villages *mata* is the presiding deity of the village while in some villages Bhairam or Burha deo is the presiding deity. Besides Mata and Bhairam there is another powerful deity namely Dand deo.

The places of god and goddess in the villages are located sometimes within the habitation area and sometimes in the outskirt of the village. They are worshipped in time throughout the year. Apart from this, during annual Mandai/Marai festival these gods and goddesses are worshipped communally in the village. It is observed that gods and goddesses of all the villages under a *pargana* are taken to their *pargana* head quarter and are worshipped during Marai festival. The Marai festival of Baragaon pargana (Bhatra dominated area) is held at Karpawand. On this occasion a fair is held there with pomp and éclat. However, the representative gods and goddesses of all the *pargana* of Bastar meet once in a year during Dusehra festival at Jagdalpur, Bastar, where the representatives of various *pargana* or village gods and goddess are found either in the form of *Chhata* or *lathi* with a flag.

Apart from this there is another occasional festival known as Bali festival. Since this festival is very much expensive, they perform once in 5 or 10 or 15 years. In *Bali Jagar,* god Bhima and his wife Kondni are worshipped. The worship continues for about a month. This ritual has various facets like Lakshmi Jagar described earlier. Bali is the ritual for agricultural activities among the Bhatra. Apart from this Bhatra also observed and participated in certain other Hindu festivals like Goncha (Chariot), Siv ratri (worship of Lord Mahadev), Holi, Satya Narayan Katha, Ganesh Chaturthi and keeping *tulsi* (sacred basil) plant in the courtyard.

Bhagat lok

Some among the Bhatra are converted into Satya Mahima Dharma. This conversion is a kind of social mobility movement. The Bhagat lok followers among the Bhatra are vegetarian and claim superior status over Jagatlok. It is also observed that some Mahara castes are also converted into Bhagatlok. It is also reported that originally their Gurus came from Gurundagadi village of Dhenkanal district of Orissa.

The Bhagat lok worship only one formless supreme god – *Alekh Mahaprabhu.* They wear saffron coloured cloth. They get up early in the morning and take bath. They pay *darshan* (prayer before the supreme god) twice in a day. In the morning they face the east and lie flat or kowtow seven times while in the evening they face the west and kowtow for five times. They take dinner before sunset. They don't kill animal, insects and abstain from liquor. They perform *hom* (sacred fire). They have faith on their preceptor who performs *hom* on their behalf at Gurundagadi in the month of Magh. They chant devotional songs. They do not wear leather shoes, do not worship any village deity, family deity, deity of *deogotia* and ancestral *duma* (soul). Even they do not pay any regard to the *pujari.* They pay regards to their supreme god and remember him asking his favour at the outset of any activity. They perform *yajna* under the supervision of their *guru.* An annual *yajna* is performed at their natal place – Gurundagadi on the day of fullmoon in the month of Magh (Jan-Feb). They have faith that their gurus possess power of cure from any ailment. They do not have any faith in *sirha,* do not encourage worship of the Hindu god, goddess and or participation in fairs and festivals.

It is also reported that they do not recognize any hierarchy of social division among the endogamous division of Jagatlok Bhatra sect. A boy of Bhagat lok may marry a girl belonging to Jagat lok but condition is that she must be converted before performance of marriage. Both Jagat lok and Bhagat lok followers piercc ear before marriage while Jagat lok followers of Bhatra wear *janeoi* (sacred thread) but the Bhagat lok do not believe is such *janeoi.*

III

From the above discussion it can be stated that the subsistence sector among the tribal groups has been changing towards market economy for which they are now inclined towards production of cash crops. The economic disparity among the tribe often creates rank determination. (Sarkar and Dasgupta, 2005). If we see the whole situation from Marxist angle, the process of tribal differentiation is from tribe to class, mainly peasantry. According to them the homogeneity of the tribal society is a myth and not reality. The tribe always had some kind of primordial infrastructure of social differentiation. During British period and feudal India there was gross uneven land distribution among tribes. Therefore, tribal differentiation is not from tribe to caste, rather it is from tribe to class; while, according to non-Marxist opinion the process of social differentiation among the tribal groups is a continuum from tribe to caste. By adopting the attributes of sanskritisation the tribal groups are achieving the corresponding status of caste (Aurora, 1972; Bailey, 1960; Bose, 1947 etc.). Considering the empirical data authors are of opinion that due to introduction of massive industrialization, communication system and impact of tenets of globalization in this area they will give rise to class structure in near future.

Chapter-8

Observation and Conclusion

It reveals from the aforesaid discussion that the Bastar tribes have a unique religious world of their own which often cut across their ethnic boundary and gets assimilated with the religious norms of their immediate Hindu neighbour. It can also be said from close observation that **Pat deo** or **Anga deo** – a male deity, is one of the regional chief deity or a famous deity in the little tradition of Bastar, who is often equated with Mahadev or Siva. He is regarded as *baba* and in villages of Bastar he is regarded as a symbol of Siva. [From historical account it also reveals that the whole of Chhattishgarh was under the influence of Saiva. It is observed that the kings of Pandu dynasty during 8th or 9th century were patrons of Saivaism; they were devotees of Siva and gradually it spread even to Bastar]. In this log deity one-half lunar symbol with a snake of silver or copper is embedded which is also found in **Siva linga** of great tradition. The **Pat deo**, is equally accepted by all the people of Bastar, who eradicate evil spirits (Jagadalpuri, 2003).

Bastar, in fact, had been a stronghold of Saivaism from time immemorial. This aspect was fully exploited by the founders of the Bastar dynasty who fled from Warangal with an idol of their tutelary family deity – Danteshwari/ Maoli – an incarnation of Durga and installed it at Dantewada and also declared himself as a chief priest of

Danteshwari. By declaring themselves as the prime worshipper of Danteshwari, "the kings of Bastar could integrate the tribal population of Bastar with the state. As stated above, the animistic religion of Bastar had already possessed the 'mata cult' complex in different names shades and hues such as **Maoli mata**, **Bhandarin mata, Pardeshin Mata**, **Jaliniburi mata, Telangin Mata** etc. The cult of deities is inseparably woven with the cultural fabric of the tribal Bastar. The tribal social organization is linked closely with the kinship organization found among the deities – smaller villages are the seats of secondary and tertiary relatives of a more prominent deity who is housed in another village and become a nucleii of a bunch of villages. It can be illustrated in the following manner.

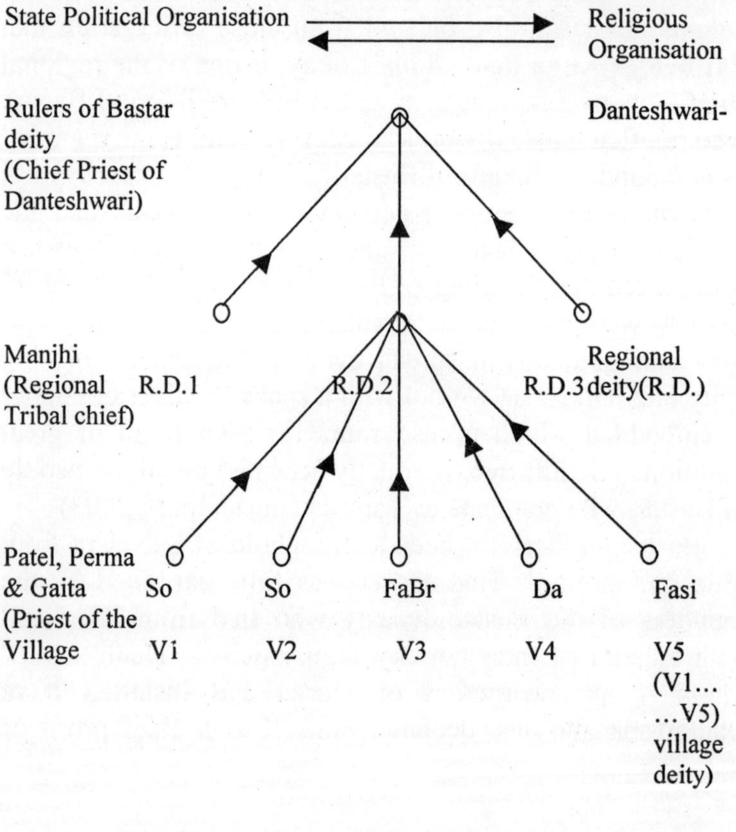

In the above illustration it has been shown that v1, v2, v3, v4,v5 are villages having their own deities who are related in turn with R.D.2 which is regional deity and similarly R.D.1 and R.D3 are other regional deities forming separate cluster of villges. Each of the regional deities is the various manifestations of **Danteshwari mata**.

Looking at the process of state formation in Bastar it has been observed that by becoming the *purohit* or chief priest, the Rajput kings of Bastar carved out a religio-political niche for themselves to which they remained inseparably attached till the last king-cum-priest-Pravir Chandra Banjdeo was assassinated in 1965. The political control of the ex-rulers of Bastar ran more or less parallel with the religious organization.

Dusehra festival on the other hand clearly signifies that it is an "integration rather than displacement of tribal elements in the development of 'nuclear areas' of sub-regional power. Ultimately, it was the fusion which helped legitimize rule in these areas." (Sunder, 1997).

It can also be said from the empirical observation on Dusehra festival that within the agricultural mode of producation, the Dusehra is an extension of the village *jatra*(sacrifice) – local festivals necessary to preserve fertility and avoid sickness. According to Dubey and Mohril (1961) **Kachan gudi** ritual is claimed to be a fertility ritual. To them, **Kachan** being an earth goddess associated with fertility and reproduction and song sung by the *gurumaya* women. According to Panika priest, a Panika sorceror helped a childless queen to conceive and in return she was asked to pray to **Kachan devi**, who is a symbol of prosperity.

The contextual, date also suggests that the king was seen as necessary for the performance of this Dusehra function for the interest of his kingdom. Induction of various roles assigned to specific ethnic groups as participants and contributors to the Dusehra ceremonies, the Royal family simultaneously ensuring their contribution in terms of revenue, administration and control even at grass root level for sustenance which makes them cohesive have helped in the adaptation and adjustment and synthesis of cultural behaviour between two or more ethnic groups which ultimately leads towards harmonious environment in the region.

The annual ritual during Dusehra since 1906 – the '**Muria Darbar' / 'Manjhi Darbar**' – wherein the tribal or village chiefs (**Manjhi** or **Chalki**) are allowed freely to speak about their problem in the village regarding agricultural practices, land irrigation, forest and its resources, wages of labour, drinking water facility, induction of developmental activities in their area, and unemployment vis-à-vis rise of Naxalites etc. A kind of promise is assured from the ruler of Bastar who would do everything in his power to alleviate the sufferings of his subalterns.

This integrated system of political control which remained intact till 1965 – the last ruler of Bastar and after his death the system is gradually weakened, though present democratic government has not been able to maintain the same degree of cohesion between the rulers and the ruled as it existed earlier. Dusehra of Bastar in other words may be termed as a meeting place for gods and goddesses as well as various ethnic groups on a larger scale. During 2004 altogether 88 **Parganas** / Village gods and goddess who are in most cases genealogically related in their celestial world, were invited at Jagdalpur who were represented at Jagdalpur by a silver umbrella (*chatta*) or *lathi* etc. In this regard Sundar (2001) observed that the ritual division of labour between different groups for Dusehra speaks of different lineages involved in the propitiation of village gods. The whole Dusehra ritual may be identified as a royal or political ritualistic activity, which acts as a cohesive nt of Bastar state. Here religious activities were shaped through the demands of state legitimacy or "in other words, how royal hegemony has been dependent on the appropriation of popular religion" (Sundar, 2001). It is also reported that the priest of all the temples of Jagdalpur were headed by non-Brahman or low caste and gradually within the past few years specially after independence these are replaced by Brahmans only.

From the aforesaid discussion it is revealed that –

(i) the whole Dusehra ritual process is a kind of little tradition which becomes a part of great tradition when in such ritual Brahman service is inducted and recitation of **Chandi** during *Navaratri* session and link the Danteshwari with **Devi Durga** of great tradition by also putting some arms and weapons in her hand which are typically vedic in nature.

(ii) Dusehra festival of Bastar has both sacred and secular elements in it.

(iii) The whole process of ritualistic behaviour is a kind of **cultural osmosis** where ethnic as well as religious boundary is not a decision making factor.

(iv) The mother cult – **Danteshwari** acts like a centripetal force where both Hindus and tribals are roaming from apex to center. It has tremendous attractive force, which one can realize through **empathy;** because in their mind if **Danteshwari** is not appeased, people of the state will become restless, starved, ill, so the subalterns of Bastar worship her. She is the supreme in the heavenly world of Bastar people. Her dictum is final and she controls her subalterns through the dreams of chief priest since now the position of king is simply ritual.

(v) To our opinion the essence of Bastar Dusehra is unique in the country and evolved as a way of consolidating political power (through **Manjhi**,

Chalki, **Patel, Gaita** etc.) using cultural and religious symbols through **Danteshwari Mata**. The various *matas* in different villages are directly or indirectly related with **Danteshwari** which clearly reflect the extent of political power of Raja (or king) to grass root level.

(vi) Thethen king of Bastar intended to involve all the ethnic groups of his states and even villages in this festivities and thus network of bondage of relationship was formed both at terrestial and celestial levels (i.e. through their deities in which they have a strong supernatural belief).

(vii) The political connotation of the festival is most evident towards the end of the festivals. On the performance of **Muria Darbar** where all tribal /parganas chiefs or **Manjhi** voice their grievances and problems at the **Darbar**. Earlier it was presided by the king but now-a-days it is presided by District administration.

(viii) The influence of Chhattisgarhi language is very low among the studied groups of Bastar.

Thus, above picture clearly reflects that in the interest of political power various ethnic groups were assigned to perform certain specific and important roles during Dusehra, which is still continuing and thereby assimilation as well as synthesis of cultural traits between two or more ethnic groups has occurred. This is certainly a product of acculturation.

Bibliography

Appadurai A. 1991 'Global Ethnoscapes : Notes and Querries for a Transnational Anthropology' in R. Fox (ed) *Recapturing Anthropology : Working in the Present,* Santa Fe : School of American Research Press

Aurora, G.S. 1972 *Tribe – Caste – Class encounters,* Hyderabad. Administrative Staff College of India

Bailey, F.G. 1960 *Tribe – Caste and Nation : A study of Political Activity and Political Change in Highland Orissa,* Manchester : Manchester University Press

Banerjee, Biswanath 1968 "The Habitat and Culture of Primitive Hill People of India, 21st International Geographical Congress, India

Banerjee, H.N. 1990 *Introducing Social and Cultural Anthropology*, Calcutta : Kitab Mahal Agencies.

Banerjee, Partha S. 2003 'In Bastar, It's different, *The Statesman* (Newspaper, 8th November, Saturday, 2003.

Bernard Alan & Jonathan Spencer (edited) 1998 'Syncretism', in *Enclyopedia of Social and Cultural Anthropology*, London & New York : Roultedge

Bhatt, Vikash 1983 'A Baba in Bastar' in *Tribal Movements in India*, Vol.2 ed. By

K.S. Singh, Vol.2, New Delhi : Manohar (pp.223-241)

Bose, N.K. 1941 'Hindu Method of Tribal Absorption', *Man in India*, Vol.27.

Bose, N.K.(reprint) 1977 'The Hindu Method of Tribal Absorption' in *Culture and Society* in *India*, Bombay : Asia Publishing House (First Published in 1941 in Science and Culture)

Chapman, R.A.B. 1898 *Political Agents notes* (Unpublished manuscript in Jagdalpur, Records Room, Bastar District, Chhattisgarh).

Comaroff, J. 1985 *Body of Power, Spirit of Resistance: The Cultural and History of a South African People*, Chicago: University of Chicago Press

Cornford, Francis 1957 *From Religion to Philosophy*, New York : Harper

Das, N.K. 1974 "A Note on Tribal unrest in Bastar", *Samatat*, Vol.5, No.4, p.31(A bilingual Quarterly)

Dasgupta Samira & Amitabha Sarkar 2003 "Synthesis of Tribal Religion and Hindu Cults in Bastar" in N.K. Das (ed.) *Culture, Religion and Philosophy : Critical Studies in Syncretism and Inter – Faith Harmony*, Jaipur : Rawat Publications.

Dasgupta, Samira 1994 *Birjia : Society and Culture (A study in Cultural Ecological Perspective),* Calcutta : Firma KLM Pvt. Ltd.

Davis, Kingsley 1966 *Human Society*, New York : Macmillan Co.

Dubey, K.C. and M.G. Mohril 1961 *Fairs and Festivals of Madhya Pradesh*, Census of India.

Durkheim, E 1954 Elementary forms of the Religious Life, trans. By Joseph Ward Swain, Glencoe I I I : The Free Press

Firth, Raymond 1996 *Religion: a Humanist Intrepretation*, London and New York : Routledge

Glasfurd, C.L.R. 1862 *Report on the Dependence Bastar* (Record Room, Jagdalpur)

Gregory, C.A. & Harihar Vaishnav 2003 *Lachmi Jagar : Gurumai Sukdai's Story of the Bastar Rice Goddess*, Austrialia and Kondagaon : Kaksad Publication.

Grigson, Sir Wilfred 1991 *The Maria Gonds of Bastar*, Delhi : Oxford University Press. Vanya Prakashan (reprinted).

Herskovits,M. 1941 *The Myth of the Negro Past*, New York : Harper & Brothers.

Jagdalpuri Lala 2003 *Bastar – Lok (Kala – Sanskriti Prasangha),* Jagdalpur : Akrati Sansthan (in Hindi)

Jay, Edward, J. 1970 A Tribal village of Middle India, Calcutta : Anthropological Survey of India.

Joshi, M.P. 1986 'Religious History of Uttarakhand : Sources and Materials, in *Ecology, Economy and Religion of Himalaya*, ed., L.P. Vidyarthi and Makhan Jha, Delhi : Orient Publication.

Lessa, William, A. & Evon Z. Vogt. 1965 *Reader in Comparative Religion : An anthropological Approach,* New York : Harper & Row Publishers

Lowie, Robert 1924 *Primitive Religion*, New York : Boni & Liveright

Malinowski, B. 1948 *Magic, Science and Religion and other Essays*,

Marett, R.R. 1909 *The Treshhold of Religion*

Mead, Goerge Herbert 1934 *Mind, Self and Society*, Chicago : University of Chicago Press (pp.296)

O'dea, Thomas F. 1969 *The Sociology of Religion*, New Delhi : Prentice-Hall of India Private Limited.

Radcliffe Borwn, A.R. 1935 'On the Concept of Functionalism in the Social Sciences', *American Anthropologist*, Vol.37

Risley, Herbert(reprint) 1969 *The People of India*, 2nd edition, edited by W.C. Rooke, Delhi: Oriental Books Reprint Corporation.

Rosaldo, R. 1989 *Culture and Truth : The Remaking of Social Analysis*, Boston : Beacon Press.

Russel and Hiralal (reprint) 1975 *Tribes and Castes of the Central Provinces of Inida*, Delhi : Cosmo Publication (First Published in 1916)

Sarkar, Amitabha & Samira Dasgupta 1996 *Spectrum of Tribal Bastar*, Delhi : Agam Kala Prakashan.

Sarkar, Amitabha & Samira Dasgupta 2000 "Religious Beliefs and Practices of Tribal Bastar : A Prelude". In M.C. Behera (ed.) Tribal Religion : Change and Continuity, Delhi : Commonwealth

Sarkar, Amitabha 1994 *Dhodia : Industrialisation and Change in a Primitive Community,* New Delhi : Gyan Publishing House.

Sarkar, Amitabha & Samira Dasgupta 2005 'Social Stratification of Bastar Tribes', *Man in India*, Vol.85. No.3-4.

Sarkar, J.K. 1986 *Social Mobility in Tribal Madhya Pradesh*, Delhi : B.R. Publishing Corporation.

Singh Deo, R.C. 1984 *Bastar Development Plan, Bhopal* : State Planning Board, Govt. of Madhya Pradesh (Cyclostyled).

Singh, Ajit K. 1982 *Tribal Festivals of Bihar : A Functional Analysis*, New Delhi : Concept Publishing Company.

Singh, K.S. 1983 *Tribal Movements in India,* Vol.2, New Delhi, Manohar Publication.

Sinha S.C. 1962 "State Formation and Rajput Myth in Tribal Central India" Man in India, Vol.42.

Sinha, S.C. 1980 'Tribes and Indian Civilisation : A Perspective", *Man in India*, Vol.60.

Srinivas, M.N. 1962 *Caste in Modern India* : Bombay : Asia Publishing House.

Srinivas, M.N. 1952 *Religion and Society among the Coorg of South India*, Delhi : Oxford University Press.

Sundar, Nandini 1997 *Subalterns and Sovereigns : An anthropological History of Bastar, 1854-1996*, Delhi : Oxford University Press.

Sundar, Nandini 2001 Religion and Culture in Bastar : The Politics of Conversion, in *The Eastern Anthropologist,* Vol.53, No.3-4.

Tylor E.B. 1871 *Primitive Culture*, London:John Murray.

Wach, Joachim 1944 *The Sociology of Religion*, Chicago: University of Chicago Press

Weber, Max 1963 *The Sociology of Religion*, Boston : Beacon Press

Xaxa, Virginius 1999 "Transformation of Tribes in India: Terms of Discource", in *Economic and Political Weekly*. Vol. XXXIV, No.24, June 12-18, pp.1519-1524.

INDEX

ETHNIC MAP OF BASTAR DISTRICT

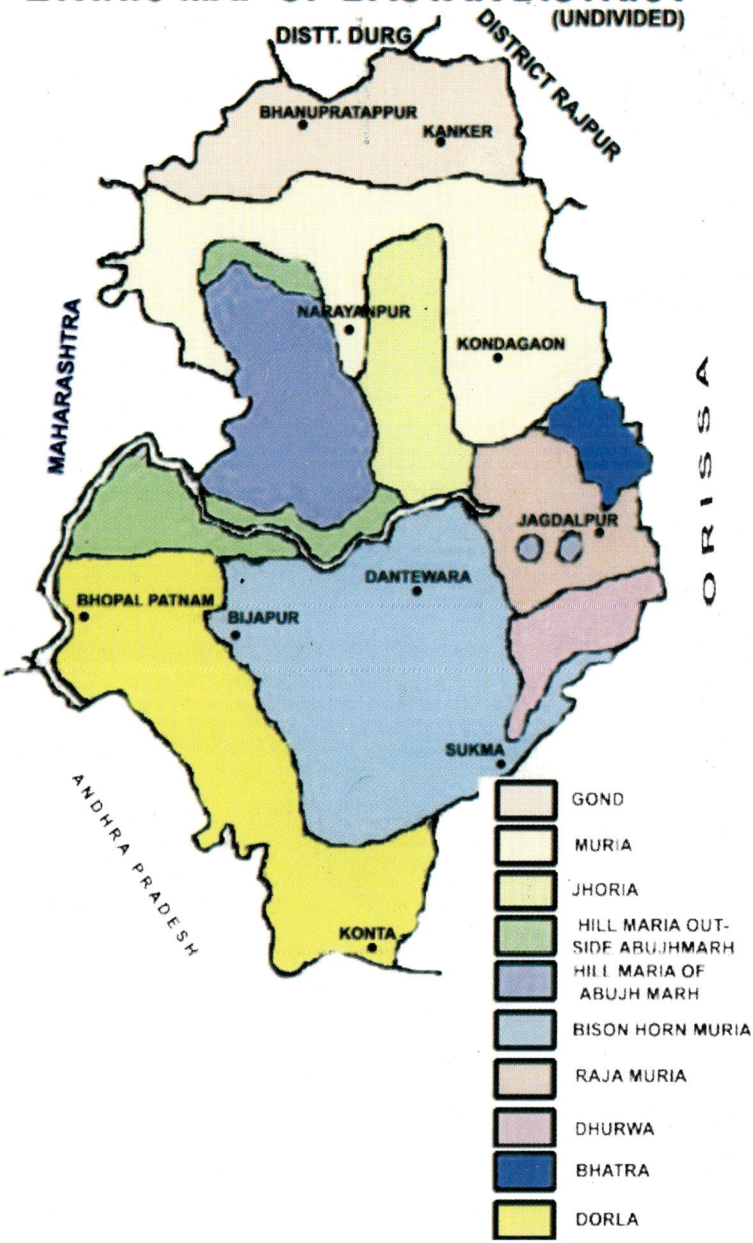

Danteshwari Ma- the tutelary deity of Bastar King

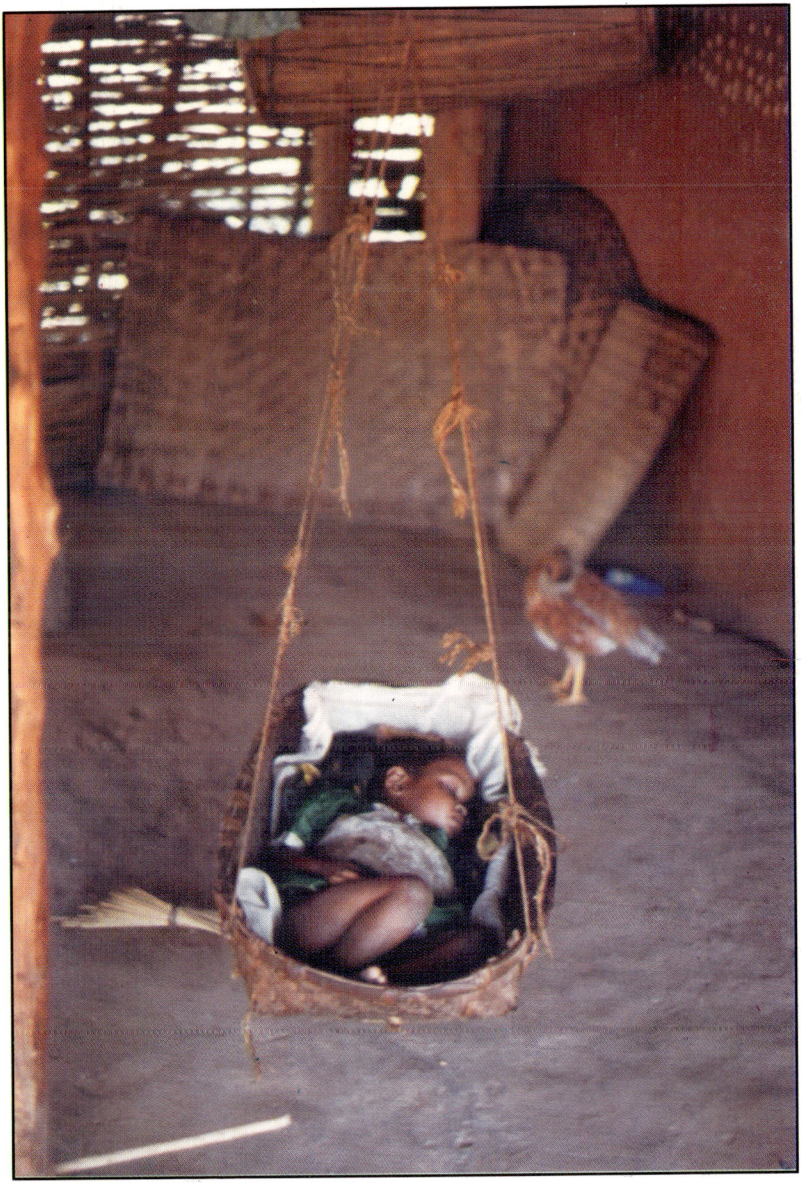

Dandami Maria child under care

Dhurwa in action

Dorla House type

On the way to market with tendu leaves

On the way to home after collection of fuel wood

Dandami Maria in dancing posture

Erabore village- Dorla Toddy trapper

In quest of food -Collection of Minor forest produce

Pat deo-Procession of Log God

Palace of Bastar King at Jagdalpur

Present King of Bastar

Dusehra Rath

Dusehra Rath

Assembly of Chhata-the representative of Pargana clan God

Assembly of tribals during Dusehra with traditional attire

Muria Darbar-Assembly of Manjhi,Chalki,Patel

Bhagat lok Bhatra at Dusehra festival

Lakshmi jagar ritual

Quench of thirst through Haria at weekly market

Swing with nails-the seat of possessed sirha at Asnar(Orcha) village shrine